MORTALITY

ALSO BY KWAME DAWES AND JOHN KINSELLA

Speak from Here to There
A New Beginning
Tangling with the Epic
In the Name of Our Families
unHistory

JOHN KINSELLA & KWAME DAWES

MORTALITY

PEEPAL TREE

First published in Great Britain in 2024
Peepal Tree Press Ltd
17 King's Avenue
Leeds LS6 1QS
UK

© Kwame Dawes 2024
© John Kinsella 2024

All rights reserved
No part of this publication may be
reproduced or transmitted in any form
without permission

ISBN 13: 9781845235932

INDEX OF FIRST LINES

All the odd numbered poems are by John Kinsella (JK). All the even numbered poems are by Kwame Dawes (KD).

1. I was nearly killed by a broken York gum limb	9
2. There were no tears, but as is the commotion	11
3. A Common Frog calls across the botanical gardens	13
4. The blue clerk declared the redundancy of God,	14
5. I wonder if we'd understand if there weren't records	15
6. At the edge of a new year, I have forgotten	17
7. What can I expect to change through teaching	19
8. I know now that the blue clerk sees blue skies	20
9. Relatively speaking... an expression that has always	21
10. In Laredo, Texas, where the brown river defies borders	23
11. Yes, what is heard, who is doing the hearing.	25
12. Outside, the snow falls steadily	27
13. Strangely – though how can it be truly	29
14. Here in the armpit of America, no one says spring	30
15. Here are the chaffinches we saw crossing the road	31
16. The asthmatic snore of the AC all night	32
17. There *are* no first elegists, *were* there?	33
18. Robert Johnson walked to the crossroads	34
19. I was thinking about the emptiness of 'celebrity'	35
20. He is a better man than me – if they come	37
21. Classes cancelled the other day.	39
22. Every day the crows stripped leaves into end	40
23. Something I missed. Not about subjects	41
24. It is May and it has come to this	42
25. A friend was calling me from death	43
26. I misplaced my woollen black Big Red tagged hat	44
27. I found a typo on a dedication page	45
28. It may be the fever	47
29. There's a severe weather warning	48
30. Yes, I'll say you're a woman. You always rise	49
31. I am wondering about messengers.	50

32. This storm of message and nostalgia beats the cage	51
33. There's another mouse "plague" on here,	52
34. From a drone's peace-loving gaze	54
35. We travel far from where we knew people	56
36. Hannah of suburbia, her speech like glass, is good,	57
37. Passing through a field can be more isolating	58
38. At twelve, I monumentalized the towers	59
39. I have been arguing both sides of mimesis	60
40. As if saying it is madness, a chemical imbalance	62
41. I have been taken apart like a weapon	65
42. Philip Larkin sings of the n-ggers, of the n-ggers	67
43. You see, Kwame, I think Larkin a shitty poet	71
44. The words are clinical, they say to her, "Buy	74
45. The first operation wasn't a success.	75
46. I propose that joy is the aborted thought. Rude?	76
47. I was worried about the local crops	77
48. How do I explain the way that a certain cult of kindness	78
49. Something *good* from the realm of settler	80
50. And this little tendon strain	81
51. I expect changes in the body	84
52. I imagine my prologue would be where fear ended	86
53. I kept two scrapbooks of space exploration	87
54. We did not choose the country or epoch	88
55. Peace is more radical than all the conjuring	89
56. After the rituals of travel – the vaccinations, the visas,	90
57. Tim has been telling me about Accra since he was six	91
58. Travelling again, I am running into	92
59. We are still close to home, Kwame,	94
60. You are rehearsing my death again	96
61. A young and record-seeking sailor's yacht	97
62. How sadly mundane seems his life despite	98
63. Through the burn, light diminishes	99
64. Anyidoho, the prof moves with a slow shuffle	100
65. My father has been taken to the acute ward.	102
66. The landscape rises noisily at the Cape of Good Hope	104
67. In this to & fro of ours, Kwame, of such long	106

68. Then one morning, three weeks after the dance	108
69. There's a big poem I want to write after the river	109
70. There are those like us who seek to bless	110
71. I am walking from the bus stop to the flat	111
72. The famous singer – the mouth of gravel	112
73. I have been troubling over poems	114
74. Oh dear friend, what have we done	116
75. Here's the strangest thing, Kwame,	117
76. I can say what I want, you can say what you want	119
77. How we step across those chasms or fall	120
78. Thrice this week, I must send condolences	122
79. My father is dying	123
80. I stay bated all week as if waiting for the flue	124
81. I do not know how to write an elegy for a teenager	125
82. Eventually what remains is all head, the sculpted	126
83. The crisis of this land	127
84. Mid-November and the air is brittle, the cold	129
85. New neighbours down the road	131
86. The blind poet still has the dog,	133
87. This is a day when your 'being out there'	134
88. I became handsome, irresistible,	135
89. I think of myself as being of one place	137
90. With care and an improvisational hunger	138
91. It is many years since we've been down	141

1.

I was nearly killed by a broken York gum limb
this morning, Kwame. Really, it was the top
third of the trunk that had snapped
in the extreme heat. Christmas day here
was forty-six degrees centigrade. Tim
saw the tree snap under the weight
of its oil-heavy foliage, brittle
in its old bones. I heard the crack,
and guessed. So, this morning, I went
out before the extreme heat came on –
though it has now come on and actually
came on when I was sawing off limbs
to free the trunk heavily teetering
with contradictions on a steep slope…
I'd planned my retreat, being obsessed
with angles, but didn't see a sharp stump
under a garland of dried grass, and as
the trunk gave way to find a more secure
resting place and I quickly backed away,
I went over and tumbled – cut and bruised
but not impaled. I pause, writing this exordium,
to remove another splinter. I can't interpret
the signs of every insect and bird, nor of the monitor
that rushed away searching for an alternative arbour,
but my loss was instantly accommodated
by all that registers as the collective "nature",
I am sure, I am sure being grounded and slightly
stunned… immobile; I sat in the aftermath
as the sun shifted the focus more, then shifted
the tenses and spatial co-ordinates of "day".
It would be glib of me to say that I was *fine*
with it "all" – for me – ending that way,
but for a moment, I had let go, and had to haul
myself back up. Affirmation! Tracy said it was wrong

of me to go off and do something like that
without letting someone know what I was
up to. *It's not the first time. Mea culpa*
has become a bit of a mantra in the way
I negotiate the rupture between nature… and *nature*.
There is a lot of grief on the eviscerated air,
and I felt its roots, its brittle air-roots
in dry air that dries away life.
But I am here, and I am writing,
and I have rehydrated myself,
though I wouldn't call it reminiscence.

JK

2.

Fish, serpent, egg and scorpion

For Kekeli

For everyone who asks receives; he who seeks finds; and to him who knocks, the door will be opened. What father among you, if his son asks for a fish, will give him a snake instead? Or if he asks for an egg, will give him a scorpion?
— Luke 10-12

There were no tears, but in the commotion
of these emotional days, the impetus for tears,
when I said to him there in the cold street,
wearing our sporty winter jackets, "I am your gift,
this body before you, still here to say, *Let's take a walk son,*
me, this complex of secure love. I am not
your enemy, not a murky pond of dangers. Don't you
know that when I was your age, my hunger
for a shelter in a man's heart was already dust?
He was dead, gone, and all I had
was the surrogates of his letters, the clues
of a narrative of love in his fiction and poems,
the snippets of affection in his old friends –
hardly enough – but all I had upon which to build
an edifice of meaning. And I wrote then,
World, world, world, that I have lost – full of every
melodrama of mourning, though it was never
hyperbole, never a lie. I said to him, "So here I am."
And my voice was phlegmy and earnest,
"Here I am for you, so use me, to feed on me,
I am your father, use me." Perhaps we all must
say this or have thought to say this, we who father
sons. Maybe. Every poem has its own ancestry,
but this was us, me embracing him, and him saying,
"Sorry dad, I know." And even now, it breaks me

that I would present him with my body,
my mortality, my leaving him; that I could let
him feel the start of his long mourning before it
has to come. I said, "I could die today," not as hyperbole,
but as a truth that runs through my veins, my lungs.
This is love, then, a father and a son, him handsome,
fluid, tender, the boy and man, all there, and me
mourning for his bereavement. It was a passing thing.
We re-entered the house with the noises of the season,
laughter, even as if that moment between us
could be set aside. Of course, we know it will not be.
I know that this father must say again and again,
"I am made for you, and I will not promise you a fish
and then hand you the threat of a serpent."

KD

3. *Tübingen*

A common frog calls across the botanical gardens
as a storm warning goes up, though the storm
is still an hour or two away. Tim and I trace
it to a pond where it is sheltering among
lilies, eyes and nostrils above water,
to dart out, retract. Day activity,
day-vocalising, are part of its raison d'être
in May, its effort to keep ahead of the grimness
while other amphibians fall to nothingness.
It's a violent storm now, and the temporality
of a sonnet cannot contain it. The gardens
are hidden from sight, and I can't conjecture
what the frog is doing beyond searching out bliss —
what we are doing with our records of loss.

JK

4. *Charged*

For Dionne Brand

The blue clerk declared the redundancy of God,
before the mind-break of war, with its flaming foil
of terror and betrayals. I retrace the funky oil
scent in her cantos, how much she cursed the rod
of the deity, before the march of politicians who trod
through that beautiful island, heavy-booted; such toil
to crush all dreams. They were formed of the same soil
of greed and lack of conviction, their feet shod
with boots slicked with meaty entrails. Never spent,
they marched through her fetid dreams wrecking things
in her tiny snow-covered cottage where she went
to recover. The voices followed. Now God springs
back at her, demanding all the credit in the bent
way that the most corrupt earn their unholy wings.

KD

5.

I wonder if we'd understand if there weren't records
to break. Record temperatures, records broken daily —
something to peg or mark our decline, an *in medias
res* accumulation of stats to distract ourselves,
as if cause and effect are difficult co-determinants.
We watched someone throw a lit cigarette
out of their car window near dry grass
on a forty-degree day and drive on faster
than flame might catch them. I am sure
their bodies tell them it's stinking hot out there,
that for weeks fires have been lit and fought,
that an ancient karri forest is gone forever.
I wonder if he'd understand more if there weren't
records to break, or if their being broken daily
has made him insensitive to consequence,
or if cause and effect are short-circuiting empathy?
I am troubled by both the danger and the indifference
to death, to mass death, Kwame, and remember
how in the early days of the Trump administration
screeds of climate data were simply deleted
so the record would look different and the hum
of industry and leisure could be maintained
without rivalry. From records. This is still today
and record after record is being broken. The day
isn't young, but there are still more records
to be created, to be created and broken. We
returned from the city after another series of tests —
a biopsy of timelines and flesh, or personal
records and the records of an increasingly
large cross-section of the population. Always
awaiting results, anxious, it reorientates
'results' into a weather chart of predictions
and facts, of greater influences and local
factors — how someone's tossed, lit cigarette

can add to the record vicariously
and directly, how love can lift
the body to cope with greater stress.

JK

6. *Inconsolable*

For John Kinsella

The classics can console. But not enough.
        — Walcott, "Sea Grapes"

At the edge of a new year, I have forgotten
my rituals of hope. Sleeplessness has deprived
me of memory, or the clarity of hope, which is
the art of the imagination — how to find joy
in what is to come. The weightiness of being
sheltered here, repeating the rituals of the span
of my life, without the interruption of new landscapes,
the calculation of bodies unfamiliar to me;
relearning the exhilaration of a different light —
we are promised none of this. Still, they showed
me the end of things, the last of the ancient trees,
the closed secret of berries and nuts, the way
we learn of the breaking open of the trunks
of trees to release hungry gases to the air.
All of this is shadow — what we must look to,
unless there are, shall we say, poems and the joy
of their making. I fear that I find no comfort
in the classics. It's because no one smells anymore
the shit, dried blood, the flies, the funk in crotches
of divination, the rank earthiness of diseased bodies,
the dirt in the nails, the spit, the acne,
the emptiness of fathers squatting in a circle,
farting, one saying his daughter's name —
Persephone, or *Demeter* — waving away flies
from his mouth of broken teeth. The body
will rot, their bodies will rot, and the flowers
they gathered are the desperation of those
fearful of the heavy stench of the middens
where the sacred menstrual cloths are discarded.

These squalid tableaux, thick with texture
and stench, are the classics that may give me comfort,
the ancients not yet transfigured by our art
into bright perfection – the whitewash of myth,
the inadequacy of the colonial's simile.
I envy you the witnessing of catastrophe's
beginning, the culprits, the unfinished cigarette
tossed, the flaming, the clue to an empty motivation –
I envy this, though I have no right to. The myths
offer no comfort, though we must make them,
for we are built for the stories of our meaning.

KD

7.

What can I expect to change through teaching
"writing environmental activism", Kwame?
Each act within the system, each addition
to an institutional architecture... *and* each undermining
of the structure, waiting for weeds to arise
and take over; it doesn't fit, any more than being
a pantheist in a secular configuration. To say,
Embrace the living, cherish roots, leaves, skin
and wings... is a subjective anomaly within
the "rigour". But before I arrived, a language teacher
wrote on the whiteboard, illustrating gerunds,
"John is gaslighting his colleagues." I am sure
it couldn't refer to me, new on the scene,
but it unsettled me, who so loves community.

JK

8. *Peace in the house of shades*

I know now that the blue clerk sees blue skies
when her eyes are closed. She lifts her face, sniffs the air
in search of the familiar. I, too, am there
haunting her through the city; her hungry eyes
are mine, but she draws soft edges in the way she lies
about what she has seen. It's easy after the flare
of the zippo light crackling the seeds. Smoke scares
away the nightmares, she tells me. "High is the prize
for my efforts, high is the peace of broken vows."
I confess her words are like the shelter of a bough
of a leaf-heavy magnolia. I watch swallows
dart and dive across the blue, then at the house
of shades, I declare myself the willing spouse
of this art, freely sprung verse, and all its hallows.

KD

9.

Relatively speaking... an expression that has always
seemed out of kilter to me. I mean, in such a short
space of time, so much damage has been done,
and so many elegists have noted and lamented
the fact, but it continues unabated. Unabated –
another one of those word-expressions that fills
in for action. Action. To be rhetorically delved
out to fill in the blanks – rhetorical as laments
that catch-all, cover all bases... general decryings
of the state of things, suitably laden with *mea
culpas*, meaning we have only so much to give
and so much to take, just to set the spirit level
bubble to a point anywhere near centred –
which it can't be. This is the point where
I refer to an incredible sighting, an affirmation
to offset the agony of realising ineffectual
utterances, of efforts amounting to nothing
by both immediate and comic reckonings.
So, what will it be? Well, it can only be
the brilliance of a rainbow bee-eater
pausing mid-air between the hesitation
marks of trees. Synced (not necessarily
with an "of course") with enacting
celebration, with family put on hold
because of a Covid alert on Christmas
day, or the delayed gathering (very small-scale)
actually taking place on New Year's day,
which has always been an empty
signifier for us (not different from days
before and days after – outside those
days being essentially different... obviously...
obviously...), not because New Year's day
substitutes, but just because it was (and is)
the only day possible, the only way

we can make our gathering happen. And then,
looking up to the mountain and realising
that on a portion of "private land"
a hit-and-run clearing of bush has taken
place. Mortality, relatively speaking,
that would have sadly brought its own
celebrations among the destroyers —
the clearers imagining their actions
entirely justified, entirely within
their scheme of things. It's sad that I am
so confident in my knowledge of this —
I have seen too many such self-congratulations
among revellers of deletion, "makers"
who say the "loss of a bit of bush
is compensated by the pleasure or leisure
or economic benefits" such actions bring. And,
in case anyone reading this wonders, it was
by following the emphasis of the rainbow bee-eater's
flight, colouring, shifting circumstances
while enjoying the company of family
that I caught sight of this latest excision,
drawing it to the attention of the others,
who sadly gathered to trace its extent, having
just been celebrating the rainbow bee-eater.

JK

10. *Theology...*

i

In Laredo, Texas, where the brown river defies borders,
the silt of centuries replenishes itself
in the cycles of ordinary existence; the wide sky
at night is the only sign of tomorrows, of history,
here where myths have filled the deepest sleep
of those ancients who have left the debris of the living:
broken pots, gleaming stones, combs, and clumps
of hair. In a home, at the edge of the new year,
a prodigal patriarch who never left, sits at the head
of the table, the feast laid out before the tribe, and he begins
the rosary of his penitence, while the children
and the children's children giggle, in the way of families,
at his sombre performance, and he explodes, the buffoon,
defining himself in his own image. The rosary
falters, and the prodigal patriarch storms out
of the hall. A small laugh. The poetess says,
"This is the fault of Cristobal Colon; look at us."

ii
for Sena

Here in Lincoln, the air is crisp, sub-zero,
and the dog will not step out. I labour moving
snow; it seems as pure as the eye
can manage. The blue of dusk is tender
as a camera can ask for. I clear the lawn,
make a tawny patch, and mark a path
for her to move with a wounded ballerina's
mincing trot. Above, the geese bark, the air cut
through with the noise of centuries – a dark
animal promise. Tomorrow, we will drive

east, hours east, through Iowa, into Chicago.
The winter has settled on us, the sunlight stunning
the world around us. These are rituals we will
carry out, a father and a daughter. Her hair
is cropped low and tinted a bronze elegance.
We will rehearse the year ahead – laughter,
along these repeating highways, a way to prayer,
and she is the laugh and I am the laugher.
And the Listener will overhear our laughter.
It is all we ask of the Listener, these days.
We require only a distracted and slant attentiveness.
The rest is not our business, dear Lord.

KD

11.

Yes, what is heard, who is doing the hearing?
Is this listening? I hear pictures and trace sounds
in the dirt. We have just returned from a few
days in Geraldton, where I went to high school.
Four hundred and thirty ks north of here
on the coast; it is such different country.
We met my brother by the sea and talked
for ages; we met our friend Charmaine
and her son by the sea and talked for ages.
And Charmaine invited us to her place
on our way back home the following morning,
and we yarned towards the bright blue
of midday. The stories we heard were
the stories of country and heritage
and we grew in the hearing and seeing.
Not my stories to tell, but I cherish
the memory; only yesterday, but their
time stretches in all directions forever
and shifts the nature of memory into
something that goes forward and back,
that is always travelling sideways,
that is always enhancing and defining,
always searching for the best way through,
for answers, and for what formed the questions.
From the shade, we watched the full-blown
sunlight and heard the rustling of leaves.

That snow, Kwame. That glaring snow. So far
from the glare of beach sand, from the ships
being guided in and out of the port – the strange
commerce of endgames, pulse of navigation lights.
I know the kin of that snow from our years in Ohio,
and I know its sublime tricks, its edgy purities.
One time, when I had to go down to Australia,

and a snow storm hit Gambier, and Tracy and our daughter
and baby Tim were snowed in — snow up to the windows —
Tracy had to call a student babystitter to mind the children
because the car was snowbound and she had to get
to the shops, and when she got back the student
was holding baby Tim, and Tracy, marvelling,
asked if he'd cried, and she replied, No, he
just looked so beautiful I had to have a hold.
And the snow stayed still until it called down
its companions and it snowed long again.

I hope your journey to Chicago is joyful, Kwame,
and that the laughter and the laugh merge
and echo throughout the city. I hope we hear
that snow is eternal and that the blue sky of here
is part of its understanding of world. I hope
the mortality of words enlivens them,
encourages them to ring out, so the resonances
mark destinies and origins through their zest
and urge to be. This love of conversation.
This elemental belief: matter, speech, matter, speech.
The vacuum is the fullest space — full of noise
and vibrant images. There we meet, telling
each other what's going on, how we respond.
This from the heat. And always fire too close, too close.

JK

12. *Walking...*

i

Outside, the snow falls steadily.
I know the calm of travelling
beyond these prairie lands.
I search for The Burning Spear;
Burning Spear's cosmic elegy
is the song that will not start,
as if the sorrow has pressed down hard
unspeakable lamentation
on his cantankerous soul.
Winston Rodney is no saint.
The aging reggae veterans
tell tales of his petulance – the man
before the possession of bass
on the stage – the Jonah before the whale.

"Why you throw the old man off the cliff?"
His body trembles, he hiccups
at first; we know he is priming tongues,
the way the penitent lets the words
tumble out, the mechanics of it,
the chest heaving, the throat taut.

"Why you kill the pregnant lady?
History can recall, history can recall."
And riding the sweetness of the melody,
moving sluggishly over the cloud-heavy
mountains, the question: "Do you?
Do you? Do you, remember? Do you?
Do you remember the days, the days..."

ii

I've chosen silence for the walk —
not silence but the whitewash
of a snowscape, the soft crunch
of my feet. I pray, look for the light,
look for the parts of the pavement
drenched in the sun, for the heat,
for the cellular transformation
from the sun's chemistry
in the skin. These days, I am
contemplating gifts — those I failed
to conjure during the season.
What I wish, what I wish for you,
is more mornings awaking from deep sleep,
haunted by delight, the anticipation
of a thing that has distilled itself
through drunken sleep into a deep
sensation of delight anticipated.
I wish for mornings of such
unadulterated desire and expectation.
Not the substance of it but the essence.
What we call hope, the basic gift of waiting.

[Burning Spear live in Germany, January 25th, 1981]

KD

13.   *Colonial botany*

Strangely – though how can it be truly
strange between us now, Kwame,
so long have we been making strings,
knots, loops and garlands of talk? –
I was writing of a magnolia
only a few days ago – a syllabic poem
from the spiral path of an arboretum.
I was writing of the fractious weather
intensifying the curl of flowers,
recalling holes in foliage and cultures
left by botanical collecting,
and the counterweight of perfume
to calm the troubled air, a form of work,
an incident of pause in passing, a melancholia.

JK

14. *Spring*

Here in the armpit of America, no one says spring
has arrived. It is seasonless, the sand's lush
brightness, and the startling blue. The wood thrush
has arrived, discrete in its grace. I wring
my white beach towel, let the warm water sting
the nicks on my battered toes. I've not felt the soft brush
of salt sea water on my skin, not felt the rush
of current, the pipping bubbles, the swoop and fling
of cradling waves in years – this baptism of joy.
I am teaching the line, its beginnings
and its endings, and soon everything cloys,
all this optimism about verse. It is sinning
that births great verse, I don't say. I am the boy
at the sea's edge, fearful that the world is winning.

Panama City, Florida

KD

15. *Here are ambiguities*

Here are the chaffinches we saw crossing the road dividing the forest.
Here are the blue-numbered logs we saw by the fast-flowing stream.
Here are the voles we saw moving through leaf litter, nibbling.
Here are red kites we heard high in the pines, holding down their flight.
Here are the trees that sheltered us, shedding petals and forcing out new leaves.
Here are the plastic streamers that blocked our way, fluttering over the path.
Here are the gradations of those gauge boards as the water reached up.
Here are the meadows effusing and fermenting – spontaneously erupting.
Here is the mayfly on my hand, bringing itself into synch with my biorhythms.
Here are the same steps redirected up-hill, taking so much more work – a test.
Here are horses being led by riders searching the forest for an inner light.
Here are resplendent blue beetles glowing next to a dead comrade – to grieve?
Here are blue stars evoking purple flags evoking white-winged flowers as aftermath.
Here is a record of passing as nettles vibrate and pine cones drop.

JK

16. *On kindness*

To understand the whole language
the whole immaculate language
of the ravaged world.
"Inventory" — Dionne Brand

The asthmatic snore of the AC all night
lulls me to a fitful sleep, as if held there
like a night nurse waiting for a pause, where
the deepest silence is the ending of light.
At dawn, the canvas blinds glow, pulsing bright,
and waking me to the lull I feared. The rare
gossip of birds seeps through the muggy air.

What I know of their brittle song is not quite
enough to read portents or the science of the wind.

Their immaculate language will outlast my end,
which is a strange kind of comfort, a mind-
easing epitaph for me, still living, to amend
the errata of my clumsy life. "Be kind,"
they sing, "to the sorrowing ones, to foe and friend."

KD

17. "All things are made for mortals by human toil and care."
    — Archilochus (CURFRAG.tlg-0232.15)

There *are* no first elegists, *were* there?
We seem inside the elegy, don't we?

And that's a condition of growth and bliss
as much as loss, eh? This is what I read

in the face of a tone-flower that closes
late in the day and reopens with morning.

Making elegies is work, and that might
be from inside as well. It's not a role

to be taken for granted, and it can set up
cyclical vibrations in the forest, the roof cavity.

There are no late or final elegists, are there?
Nobody is going to sign off with feet in the ear,

with histories of sailing and flight,
a reckoning of losses — the lines

that can't be retrieved from the refuse,
can they? Making own beds is not always

passing away, and a vase of extinct flowers
on the bedside table is just out of reach.

And from inside the vase, replace words
with images, perennials with annuals.

JK

18. *Eshu or Ambition*

Robert Johnson walked to the crossroads,
the place where the spirits chatter,
and there he met a large Black man, some called him Satan,
some called him Legba, some called him Blues,
but whoever he was, he took Robert Johnson's guitar,
and he played the guitar, and played it well,
and when Robert Johnson returned to the land
of the living, the small towns, the juke joints, the bars,
and the fields of elation and suffering,
he was transformed in ways that let folks know
that he left something behind with that big Black man.
There is a faint line between gratitude and loathing,
the self, turning in on itself – for what does it deserve?
And it is not even a question in search of an answer,
for the answer is as ancient as the pathologies
of desperate people in search of a cult of hubris,
elegant as a prayer, that says we cannot make
of ourselves what we are not. It bears saying,
for the sake of this art, that Robert Johnson
is me, though my triumph was to leave the crossroads
intact. No one offered me the genius of hot fingers –
I waited, and the big Black man set the guitar down,
walked away with his bowlegs and strut, tossing
back, "Dat ting is out of tune." So, there was that.
Back in the square, no one turned their faces
from the glow of me, a few polite nods,
and the dogs moved along with their doggy
life, as the ancients liked to say; and me,
I returned to my hut, sat and watched the world
pass me by, my heart thick with love in search
of a home. Perhaps, this is ambition, this persistent
hunger. Today is a day of stomach cramps,
the hollow melancholia of the interim, the slough
between mountains, and this is what it must be.

KD

19.

I was thinking about the emptiness of "celebrity"
today, as people often do who aren't celebrities.
I was thinking about the astonishing hollowness
of "influencers", of social media stars whose
opinions *sell* products. I was thinking
about the nature of "opinions" and where
they connect and depart from a poetics.
I was thinking how celebrity is a kind of anti-elegy,
a claim for quantifiable immortality with little thought
for hidden death, with a spirituality of own agendas,
a personal-public own sense of worth, an arranging
the world as desired. Trump was the obvious master
of this, but he's really a distraction from its compulsion
to replicate and replace. An ontology. And sure,
it's never completely as it seems, but product revenue
is product revenue, and analytics are *reality*.
From outside, we might declare it temporary.
No great revelation, but it's literally what
I was thinking just before I read your beautiful
antithesis, Kwame, antithesis of celebrity
in the alternative true story of Robert Johnson,
in your grace of amanuenses. A tuning fork.
I have, in my own limited way, actually
tried to travel alongside Johnson
for over forty years, but he has taken no notice
of my attempts to insinuate myself into his music,
to lift out of pits of despond with the "Terraplane Blues".
It's a long and tangled personal story without
followers and influence, and with too many arrivals
and departures. It's over-stuffed with imitation and awe,
and that's at least part of the problem, but it's
also distress at the new heads and old shoulders
of the white music industry and its *tried tested true*
exploitations of class and heritage. I think I can hear

the mis-tunings of your guitar as true tunings, Kwame;
I think I can hear the notes some might not
want to hear. Or is this just an errant note heard
at the Crossroads? In my one-way conversations
with the music of locales that are not my locales,
with music that attracts me but doesn't want
or need me in any way, I remember
warnings about never touching bags blowing
at crossroads on Réunion island – never
to pick up unless you want to risk
catching a bad spirit. But even now,
I pause before moving on, and hesitate to describe
what I hear, though I am moved to my core – it's likely
(very likely) nothing to do with a stranger like me,
likely none of my damned business,
and there are sets of notes
that are not mine to remember.

JK

20.

All summer the devil
was sharping his blade
on cold black whetstone
& now this hard rain
falling inside, turning life
into gray moss,
but I still love my jackfruit.
　　— Yusef Komunyakaa "Autobiography of my Alter Ego"

He is a better man than me – if they come,
sit on a stool in the dark, dank corner
of my art, maybe then, with the shadow
and my eyes going, I could slip and make art
of them, but you know how they are, they are so
purehearted in their bold-faced way to seek light
and hold the centre. I am not able. Or I am
just tired. It is so much work, as it is to find me,
how I have neglected myself – all the files,
all the scrawled poems thick with my concealments –
slivers and fragments and coded sorties
asking for attention, just for care.
The boxes crowd my upstairs office;
my masked clerk is sorting through the flaking
files. Occasionally, he will approach me
with an armful of manilla folders and ask:
"You or your father?" He has not yet learned
to decipher our neat handwriting, crawling
over the page. I linger, return to another time,
and the names of the dead, intimately
mentioned, come back to me. Then it all seems
sordid, the errors of affection, now the distillation
of love into a humanity. I know the value
of being seen. In these words left here casually
is the evidence of my tenderness in friendship,

the surprise of who filled my days, the colour
of our politics somehow silenced by the details
of the present problem — where to eat or when
to gym, or who is dying, or the weather.
This is how language archives a lived life.
I hand the folders back to him.
"Me," I say. And the filing continues.
I am not able, the Nigerians say in mild
exasperation, all this grammar collected
over the years; and in the end, I love
jackfruit, Komunyaka says, meaning
get thee behind me ole devil, get thee
behind me you constant visitor; meaning
I love my ordinary, given self, which is true love.

KD

21. *Strike*

Classes cancelled the other day.
I support the bus drivers
and their action – low pay
and poor conditions. The manners

of capitalism – a promise
to reduce the number
of cars on these roads; a crux
of the crisis. To infer

roads unfold into forest,
or that a carrion crow
is pursuing our rest,
isn't to validate an escrow.

A day spent writing the opposite.
A day without public transport.

JK

22. *In the clefts*

Every day the crows shred leaves into end-
notes to be kept for the great reveal. I shore
up the chaotic world with the whisper and roar
of lines I've pieced together as I wend
my way through the thorn fields and then ascend.

I do not mean to chart my life here by keeping score
of words and melodies I make, but I do pour
them all out as a way to make sense of what I spend
my days finding in the clefts of the streets of this town.

Perhaps, the great reveal will bring peace this time,
having held in escrow the hope that my uneasy crown
of sorrows will be laid to rest. I'm past my prime,
and am happy with the cliche of it. I put this down
here, this messy legacy of my essence, my rhyme.

KD

23. *topographies*

Something I missed. Not about subjects
or objects, not about roles or presences,
not about the up-drop flight of insects.
Not about any of these. *About* correspondences.
Yes, I feel sure of it. But not Baudelaire's.
Not about Paris, though we will be there
in a couple of weeks. Not about trains
or glasshouses holding tall strains
of tropical trees. Not about arid
zones I can shift into by simply
changing buildings, nor about the grid
we are connected to while being, really,
supernumerary here. That's it, isn't it? A riposte.
To correspond with *and* to what's lost.

JK

24. *Digging in Nebraska/ Nebraskan Gothic*

It is May and it has come to this. My king-
dom of parcelled out plots, the neighbour riding
his mower, the yelping dogs, the entitled cats striding
across the cropped face of grey sidewalks. A bird's wing
rots at the mouth of the grand drain, and here I swing
from underserved peace to despair after gliding
through this decade of rightful living, hiding
away all blissful filth, the vibrancy of the guilt-thing.

Picture me, rake and shovel, standing here,
an armed mid-American dreamer of a billion
points of light – that lie of that old chevalier.
I dig deep, searching for worms, and turn up blood sillion –
yes, that word's borrowed for sure, but not too dear
a price for the flame of this sinful sulphidic vermillion.

KD

25.

A friend was calling me from death
and asking to be remembered. At least
that's what I think he was doing.

I was drawing the Empyrean which seems
so much about geometry, but other
things were reconfiguring, so I said,

I owe you a poem, which I write
not so much as memorial but as
a means of communication I think

might *leap the gap*. Living, I would
never have offered you a poem that
contained "might *leap the gap*". How

much of this would be recognisable
to anyone else who knew you? Advocate
for the postmodern, we might agree

that elegy is theory as well as practice.
I am willing to take the risk in sending
this out as part of the conversation,

to say that I just heard you out of somewhere,
reminding me to have something to say —
and it was no whisper, it was a declaration.

And here it is, mate, answered — a poetics.
Can you hear the "devices"? I know you'd
never ask me to turn the volume down.

JK

26. ...Hat...

I misplaced my woollen, black, Big Red tagged hat,
my badge of mid-western belonging. I have lost things
in the dark, in my hurry to make good time;

I have misplaced things that ritual
and repetition have not enshrined in the stations
of my dailies. My hat, I have lost my hat, and it's sixteen

degrees. I say, "I can't find my hat."
"You are going to freeze," she says. It is dark,
the pre-dawn roads are empty, a comfort.

And she offers her Russian hat. "You'd look cute in it."
This is not part of the ritual. I am now the unadventurous one,
and this is a lie. Part of the burden I've placed on love.

Like all tags in love, it is a lie — a way to settle fights,
by invoking the lie of genes or something worse.
"You'd look cute in it", she says. "My Russian hat."

It's not, of course, Russian. She doesn't want to go to Russia.
I have no language for quarrels today. I am heavy
with the shadowy sorrow in this gentle gloom.

The humming car is a warm duvet, tender
as the casual embrace in half sleep, breathing, breathing.
The greying of things for no good reason.

"I dropped the hat," I say, meaning I won't say
that for the rest of the day I will be feeling tender,
my body aching as if someone else has crossed over.

Circling Chicago, the fields of snow ripple as grey
oceanic skin as far as the eye will allow. The elusive horizon
an antidote to the elegiac — the temporal sorrow.

KD

27.

I found a typo on a dedication page
and it's bothered me as typos always do,

but it's disturbed me as well. Tracy,
knowing how such things get to me,

says you'll absorb it eventually,
and I will. Time will make the correction,

however I look at it. The error is one
of certainty, of complete conviction

that the dedication stands alone,
that it entered its own time on being

written. I try to move past the error,
try to say good intention is everything,

but it still stares out at me. I return
to it compulsively, bewildered by

my failure to notice through so many
proofs — always concentrating

on the integrity of the *texts*. *And yet*,
the dedication is the purpose of those texts.

And yet, it's an obvious typo — meaning isn't lost,
but something is, even if few people notice.

The feeling of transience it brings bothers me —
that dedication was intended as a permanence.

Something is lost, and not much is gained.
I've always thought of textual glitches

as being generative. I have always
hoped that new possibilities

might arise from a genuine slip of the hand.
I apologise to the dedicatees. I won't forget,

and moving on will make me more determined
to honour and to read more closely.

JK

28.

It may be the fever —
the dark wood panels
consume all the light.

I wake to see a note.
Someone far in the tropics
tells me her dream

of bathing a child in the river
where it is cool,
to calm his fever.

Perhaps it is the contagion.
I am in half sleep,
and yet still alert.

The world of the traveller
is the world of a dream.
We sleep for so much

of our living. This sounds
like a waste, except for those of us
who understand that our bodies

are engines, and dreams
are made to feed
our days with light and hope.

We fear in dreams
and then leap
and cross the line.

Fire and sacrifice —
this is the universe
that will keep us going.

KD

29. *Theory*

There's a severe weather warning
for the southwest of Australia,
and storm cells will cross 'Jam Tree Gully'
when I am moving under beech trees
in Schönbuch nature park. Yesterday,
we were in Heidelberg where Tracy's
great grandfather went to university,
where I once read a poetry of adversity.
I am half-listening to a programme I can only
partly follow (*it's in German*) about the destruction
of antiquities in Iraq, the (re)consigning
of written language (*voices over voices*) to military
markers, the stone dust glossolalia
of archaeology and violence. Wavering strings.

JK

30. *Hurrahing obsession*

"Be not afeared this isle is full of ... sweet airs"
The Tempest

Yes, I'll say you're a woman. You always rise
to the challenge and take the charge, "bad behaviour",
for what is only a metaphor, but wavier,
something akin to empathy. You read the skies
returning to the Rock, skin tattooed, with wide eyes
desperate to consume everything. Oh, Saviour,
at Treasure Beach, I did not expect to see you, a
creature with hair full of cowries who, to all my replies,
gave an ironic chuckle of knowing, that shoulder
shrug, that sad smile, impervious to guilt — so sweet!

This is my song of delights: I am the beholder
of terrors and you asked me that next time we meet,
I should offer you sounds that won't hurt; and bolder
acts of joy, so you'll clap hands and leap to your feet.

KD

31. *Messengers*

I am wondering about messengers.
Messengers from gods, towns and institutions.
Messengers from different geographies and conditions.
Messengers who are standing in for other messengers.
I am wondering if I should send a message,
though I don't tend to 'message'. I write a note
to myself and file it under 'communications', not
'communiqués', any more than a message
from me would be a 'dispatch'. I receive
what comes in differently — but never
indifferently. Respecting the role, I defer
to the messenger's raison d'être: not to deceive.
This sounds like a world-view, even a poetics.
I interpret what wings in or out, its ascetics.

JK

32. *Caged*

Oh, my name — it ain't nothin'
My age — it means less
The country I come from
Is called the Midwest
             Bob Dylan "With God on Our Side"

This storm of message and nostalgia beats the cage
of this delicate machine, and, as they say, truth dwells
in the details. Lies run amok in this nation. They fell
from the lips of the leathered settlers from age to age,
and took root and sprouted alien forests where the stage
coaches stalled. I am tired of history, tired of the spells
it weaves around me, seeping through my skin into my cells
of terrible sorrow, until my only recourse is consuming rage.

John, I think now of the strange sensation of deep rest
I felt sitting at the sea's edge, dumbly, the warm air a nest,
a calming, and I knew then that nostalgia was a prison.
I knew that I'd return to this landlocked place where the best
to hope for would be beauty etched in the distressed
fabric of my days, and, perhaps, joy in dry bones rising.

KD

33.

There's another mouse "plague" on here,
and though we are keeping them
out of the house, they thrum
through the roof and wall cavities,

burrow into the banks
and open portals between
things we didn't know
had betweens.

Yesterday, I opened
the silver shed to the over-
whelming stench of decay —
of mousemortality.

There's so much stuff
crammed into that space
that I couldn't find the dead
mouse, and with the heat

it will reach a certain pitch
before diminishing. I wonder
how the odour affects
other mice trying

to find their footing
in a sudden mouse world.
Owls and snakes will
increase their attentions,

and past experience
suggests the mice will
peak in their breeding
then rapidly decline… tapering

off into a quieter existence,
the impression of birth
and loss bringing hesitation
as they gather, as they feed.

JK

34.

After "It Bruises"

i

Under a peace-loving drone's gaze,
purring its presence, above it all,

not seeking to startle, the drama enacts itself:
two bodies walk a mountain road towards

each other, appearing and disappearing
behind its slopes, bends and contours,

until, after the squall and the bright light
and deep shadow of moving clouds,

after an hour or so, they meet,
without fanfare, pause, and then

continue again. I know, as does
the controller thumbing the drone's throttle,

that were either of them to gaze upwards,
the sight of this object, eying them from above,

would terrify with the superiority of its farseeing eye –
the eye of the poet – and the disquiet of being

a small creature moving slowly through
the world, from shadow to light.

ii

This vision collapses into the Kingston memory
of a hawk's mothering scream,

diving towards my bare head,
the dizzying feeling tethering me to the earth.

We watch the destruction of bodies and streets
from the bloodless gaze of the drone's eye;

we make games of our terrors, nightmare
our ends in the inexorable zooming in of the eye

towards the target, towards the tower, towards the factory,
towards the church, all these continuing on a loop, again,

and numbingly again, until all terror is siphoned
from our world. I keep returning to the memory

of imagining a meeting from so far above, of
two people walking on their pilgrimages and meeting

at the point of accidental intersection, pausing,
exchanging pleasantries and prayers and blessings,

and then moving on, wondering if love,
perhaps repeated, could be the new healing.

KD

35. *For friends, and the friends we won't likely make*

We travel far from where we knew people
to find them again, to change a "setting"
and reconfigure into a different knowing.
In a square filled with samples
of distilled experience — the facade
of a church, its towers — we are overwhelmed
beyond the conventions of devotion,
shift the boundaries of accent and diction, bond
in renewed friendship. And we search for water
as the harsh sun concentrates over tents,
a makeshift presence, though an estrangement
of the city towards those without shelter
blurs the page — the homeless left to recite
their own prayers, mantras, invectives, antidotes.

JK

36. After *The Babysitter*
     for Joyce Carol Oates

Hannah of suburbia, her speech like glass, is good,
is she not, with her broken head, and her dream-thing
way to face the world; her backstory entering
our sympathy, blond and fragile, all brittle wood?
She won't be blamed, white thing, for blood in the hood,
for Zeke whose death she caused with her lies. She swings
between sad and broken without a spring
of remorse – O praise the writer's skill! What should
I do when mercy springs up in me? There's a vale
of sorrow always before me, as if the wails
of mourners and protestors still correspond
with each other, shattering the peace, sending scales
skyward. Eventually, shouldn't empathy fail?
Must I not abandon grace and blast the weak and fond?

KD

37.

Passing through a field can be more isolating
than passing through the heart of a forest.
Winding out to an edge below an incline we test
this theory by predicting the corroborating
evidence. Natural barriers have been bent
by ploughs, planting and harvests, and those
deadly shooting towers predate on shadows
becoming flesh and fur, on concomitant
ley lines that reach grazing areas
to phase through halflight, inhale
those last flashes of rising, dying stars.
Out there, even in full sunlight, we feel
vulnerable, lose our way in openness,
reach for forest, made less visible.

JK

38. *Monument*

At twelve, I monumentalized the towers
of the past: my primary school, its rounded
halls, the hollow empty classrooms where we did
sums, the sweet confusion of first lust's powers,
unspeakable dreams where my new body soured
in itself. I entered the dense gully, where, grounded
in memory, first secrets were made. My body, confounded
by dread and need, conjured warm ivory flowers.
And falling, falling, I felt the grand release
of elation and fear.
                    I declare that we are what
we do to memory to find calming peace.
I keep retelling this memory, (it is not
news), when the sky blued more, and slick with grease
in that shelter, I blessed it the holiest of holy spots.

KD

39.

I have been arguing both sides of mimesis –
always more than a copy, always less than an original,
always much in its own terms, deep in itself.

If I reach for ritual, I find there's nothing to grab onto,
though I am made from its leaves and sinews.

If I reach for ritual, I am easily overwhelmed –
I don't know what to do with its leaves and sinews.

I have been arguing both sides of mimesis –
always more than a copy, always less than an original,
always much in its own terms, deep in itself.

A tune plays in my head the wrong way
which comes out as words rather than notes.

A tune plays in my head the right way
which comes out as notes rather than words.

I have been arguing both sides of mimesis –
always more than a copy, always less than an original,
always much in its own terms, deep in itself.

Since we last spoke, a possum has taken up habitancy,
or has reminded us of our residence is at its expense.

Since we last spoke the possum has rewritten
the trees around the house and signed the iron roof.

I have been arguing both sides of mimesis –
always more than a copy, always less than an original,
always much in its own terms, deep in itself.

There have been so many losses and so many epithets.
Charcoal from old fires has been used to mark newly exposed stone.

There have been so many imbalances I have taking to lining
the house with bright dirt and dull leaves, reading stories in walls.

JK

40. *The abode of vacancy*

Babylon, yuh queendom falling,
Rahab, Ethiopia is calling...
— Peter Tosh, "Babylon Queendom"

i

As if saying it is madness, a chemical imbalance,
as if somehow the pathology of this pure lucid hatred
that makes a murderer of him exonerates a culture.

They made him. They taught him the chemical twist they call
madness. All that is abnormal is the fragility of the gate,
the latch broken – left ajar – then he murdered them.

Take back yuh chink, yuh roach and mosquito

ii

In the crowd at the station, I see my father approach
calmly, casually. His arms swing at his side,
his hands are empty, he opens them. "Armless," he says.

I have lived in cities where violence has fevered my days.
The haunting of drums in the distance – the concussion
of small artillery, the percussion of coups – fearful nights.

In another, the fear of ghosts was eclipsed by the fear
of predator gunman. The illogic of home evasions –
a boy pissing out of his window for fear of the corridor.

I learned to dismantle a .303 rifle in the ritual dance of commands:
precision and speed, the dark oil and acrid scent of weapons,
before the reassembly, the slap and rattle of ordering arms.

I run from the echo of gunfire, I have built my life around
the terror of guns. Call me a coward – I accept this – yet I live
in a country of guns, the arrogance of the armed patriots.

This is the season of righteous wars remembered, the season
of manifest destiny. I walk the neighbourhood, heart thumping,
the streets reeking of sulphur. My father's voice hums in my head.

Take back yuh chink, yuh roach and mosquito

iii

It has been a decade in this wilderness – an island of high grasses.
We have made a shelter, learned to live each day, holding close
against the soul's erosion. This is the life of one caught

in exile in the land of the bland faces, the land of stoic silence;
and each secret disclosed is a wounding, an erosion of the soul.
I walk among the fluttering flags, trying to remember the language

of my beginning, the songs that have held me content with the living
and the dead. Here I keep words that marinate in the dry heat of summer;
my prayer is that we will find a path out of here before nightfall.

Take back yuh chink, yuh roach and mosquito

iv

When I finished, I went back to the station. I washed.
Then I sat on the verandah. I drifted softly.
It was a very quiet night.

You know I am not a fugitive. Who is trying to find me?
They know where I am. You know this.
You are just a prophet who sees. You found me.

Take back yuh chink yuh roach and mosquito

KD

41. *What am I?*

I have been taken apart like a weapon
and can't be put back together —
my teenage peers expected it of me,
but I was a loner. I walked

to lose them. It's a supermoon
and a shooter is gloating — this is in
realtime, and shots are being fired.
Tim comes and asks why the explosions

are so much louder than the usual,
and I tell him it's a particularly
high-powered weapon. Large calibre,
fast bullets — likely a "professional"

roo shooter or fox hunter. They
will be about numbers and trophies,
about bounties and licenses,
and will act in the rain with disdain,

compensating for the tidal pull
of the supermoon. In this valley
you feel the shots through your bodies,
and they dismantle you even

if they leave no visible stain.
One day, a shot will stray, or find
a different way of finding a way
through. I was taken apart.

I have been teaching riddles,
and riddles without answers
are the riddles that leave
the poem intact. Percussion

and ignition, impact: detonator
and propellent, projectile.
These principles of ending
laid out as "natural" —

which ballistics would have us
lined up in sight of. Two days
ago there were roo tracks
of blood on the path outside

the house; they can't wash away
with the bands of rain. That's
what we hear: the crack and the hiss
of dampness, blood on fur,

gun oil and powder residue
that is memory or souvenir.
I have been taken apart like a weapon
and won't be put back together.

JK

42. This Violence or What to Do with Philip Larkin

Now that my ladder's gone
I must lie down where all the ladders start
In the foul rag and bone shop of the heart.
                  W.B. Yeats from "The Circus Animals' Desertion"

i

Philip Larkin sings of the n-ggers, of the n-ggers, with his
lover, Monica Jones, drunk as ever. Those butter-mouthed
Oxford types – Motion, Wilson, Amis et al. – speak with such sweet
regret for the great minor poet, as if loneliness, and liquor and all this
stuff, culminates in the vicious language of the death of the n-ggers.
"The drunker they both got, the more wildly extreme they got."
Still, they pressed record on the reel-to-reel, and sang robustly,
"God save the queen! God save the queen!"
"If one goes to the racism..." Or, "He was a man of his time..."
What does that mean? What does that mean? My father was born
in '26, so a man of Larkin's time. Larkin lived when my father lived
in his time, and I was born in 1962 and was a man of Larkin's time,
and was a n-gger still for him, like my father was an Oxon n-gger
for him, and the wound was of the time, and of this time,
and what of that? As if to say, "a man of his time" embalms
in excuses and mercy, as if to say that a lynching was a thing of its time,
while we champion his eternal genius, outside of time, beyond time.

I say to myself, "In the fifteen minutes of my brisk walk across this city,
I have considered the secrets of an existence that would consume more
pages than the hundreds and hundreds of orchestrated arias in these books,
these memoirs, these autobiographies, these biographies – all sound
and fury, signifying the dissembling of art, the lies we tell with the machine
of the tongue, that engine of the brain's tongue, the heart's tongue, the spleen.

Here's to "the whitest man I know"...*
Where did he go after the show,

after the pomp and splendour of fame,
after the port for breakfast and what's her name,
the one he captured in his fancy box camera
with her at his side, and him at the centre?

ii

Pound, Picasso and Parker, he spits, have wrecked the world,
taken us where we ought not to go, and he makes
the world — well, he wants the world made in his own
image, the dull world of secretly read books, and the jazz
he has studied and mastered, while *A Love Supreme*
smashes through his canon and, anyway, Miles does not
alliterate with the present vitriol, nor does it spit.
And this n-gger hater says jazz is his pulse,
and he is the expert on Satchmo and the big band bop,
a teenager always, with thousands of records,
colonizing the art of those he desecrates
with drunken ditties that never swing,
full of cool *yeah man's* and all that learning.
I have no patience for these contradictions;
there is no irony here. After all, it was old
as minstrelsy and the taste of collards on a Confederate tongue.
Still, one returns to the anatomy of loneliness
and the haunting persistence of his death to come.
There is nothing else there, though he slouches
his way to love's survival — such adolescent reticence.
The poet whose body of work has grown after death,
saved from the shredder and by Ms. Jones' faithful service
to the myth of him. That I envy, but only barely —
the chance to stop all the mundanity of failure
in art and words. But then I am blessed with the "biblical things",
the kit and caboodle of love and faith, and the burden
of a people in search of voice stolen from us
by his empire's greed. He ate well, son

of an accountant, the new rich, the blunt middle class,
adorer of Hitler and his order, the hater of foreigners.
And this makes poems, so many poems, come tumbling forth;
this makes the charting of my being and our being
a kind of vocation – so little space for the exquisite gloom
of his sullen solitude and Oedipal resentments.

Here's to "the whitest man I know"...
Where did he go after the show,
after the pomp and splendour of fame,
after the port for breakfast and what's her name,
the one he captured in his fancy box camera
with her at his side, and him at the centre?

iii

Viv Richards was a haunting for Larkin, cocky and chewing,
slaughtering the Brits and old Tony Gregg with his wry
shit-faced grin, his neck red with summer heat –
and the pace, oh the pace… And Larkin in Hull lamented
the end of empire. Still, are we not brothers, he and I,
for the cricket and this matter of lines after lines?
He would not be my friend, I know – and that's no revelation –
all these machinations between the wounded one
seeking a nurse, while arrogantly superior to all around.
So there is Larkin in Hull with the volume turned high,
cursing the black-wash of the empire at Lords, while Terry
Eagleton pontificates: "The blokishness was just a con",
Larkin regretting there were no "South African police to sort them out"
at the boundary, those jumping and jeering West Indian louts.

Here's to "the whitest man I know"...
Where did he go after the show,
after the pomp and splendour of fame,
after the port for breakfast and what's her name,

*the one he captured in his fancy box camera
with her at his side, and him at the centre?*

KD

* R.M. Healey at JOT101.com suggests an offensively racist poem by the sub-Kipling versifier J. Milton Hayes, a music hall act performed to music, as being the source of Larkin's line in "Sympathy in White Major" (*High Windows*, 1974). The phrase was evidently a common synonym in late 19th/ early 20th century for "doing the right thing", by playing the white man. Hayes's verse, entitled "The Whitest Man" (c. 1913) begins:

I know he's acruisin' in a pearler with a dirty nigger crew,
Abuyin' pearls and copra for a stingy Spanish Jew,
And his face is tann'd like leather 'neath a blazin' tropic Sun,
And he's workin' out a penance for the things he hasn't done.
Round the Solomons he runs, tradin' beads and castoff guns,
Buyin' pearls from grinnin' niggers, loadin copra by the ton;
And he'll bargain and he'll smile, but he's thinkin' all the while
Of the penance that he's workin' out for sins he hasn't done.

43.

i

You see, Kwame, I think Larkin a shitty poet
and a waste of mental space, but that doesn't
say anything much in itself, other than (that)

among some I know I would be shunned.
Hey, come to think of it, I'd be cancelled
by them, by those who shout loudest

against "cancel culture" as an inhibitor
of "freedoms". I don't really need
to disentangle this for anyone,

let alone you... let alone, let alone...
you know, you know... but I want to
make it clear as statement of both

solidarity and conviction. So, the doubter
or disbeliever or faith-troubled body
performs the ritual of polite worship,

and the world... disintegrates, no, it
consolidates as empires do — they adapt.
Empires and capitalism work hunky-dory,

which is something to do with *home base*
but that's not Americans in Britain (or maybe "Holland")
during the Second World War... No,

it seems nineteenth-century... not really
Larkin*esque*... esque... esque... iscus
resembling... manner of... esco-like...

wedding of souls at which the souls
make polite snarly jokes at the expense
of the uninvited, or aimed at the smattering

of invitees they are glad are not
at their tables. They might even catch
the cricket scores as bouquet – ipso facto

public display over private sentiments,
or per the poem that can do duty for marriage
or/and death – hints of one size fits – but quickly
carousing away, drunk from chosen slippers.

ii

I find some reassurance in the way fathers
can shift positions across a lifetime.
Some fathers, some lifetimes.

I spoke to mine today for the first time
in months (was going to ring… was going
to ring) to hear he's about to go into hospital

for heart surgery. At eighty-five, it's a tough call.
It was a good conversation, about footy
and friends he hasn't seen for years,

who want to be in contact. He is not a deeply
sociable man, even a loner outside family, but he
remembers those he has worked with,

and likes to keep in contact with them –
swap a letter once a year, or speak on the phone
every two years. Meet every three.

And Kwame, gee, he has changed across
the decades. A poet son is okay now.
Another son is married to someone

outside his cultural register, outside
his geography, and he holds her
in very high regard. His third son

is keeping out of strife, and is working
again after his last stretch in jail, and that's
to be proud of. Things have shifted for Dad

and will shift further when he goes under anaesthetic,
his heart handed over to a machine. He trusts
the mechanical. He was trained

as a motor mechanic, and a good mechanic
can get out of a fix with the most basic
tools. In this is a very private

and particular version of faith.
I would never ask about it, but know
it's there — much more than *suspect*.

He'd have nothing in common with Larkin,
and he doesn't read poetry beyond maybe scanning
a few of my lines in the newspaper. But

he knows it's done something for me,
and he has watched me change in my own ways
via it over the years. We are both sober. And closer.

44. *Apocryphal*

The words are clinical, they say to her, "Buy
this story of my broken history; my scar is my best
trait; it tells everyone that beauty is pressed
from the ugly marks of ancestry…" Then, her reply

is casual, a passing nod. In books things fly
about, then float away, leaving plot and character. The rest
slips away like dreams. Then we meet, move, self-instressed,
as if there are no new answers for the why

of her. The perfection of her body and face
are her protection. Her eyes search, as if deep in her vein,
she does not exist without being seen. There's a naked grace
in the casual glances — benign disinterest she meets again
and again. Her arm moves to fan away flies. Then my eyes trace
the scar, a henna ladder, her most sacred of stains!

KD

45. *Father*

The first operation wasn't a success.
And this, a couple of years after the stroke.
First operation re-routing and reworking arteries
with veins and stents, but a nerve hit so the tongue turns back
into itself, unable to make words. Relapse after relapse.
I try to chart the best way to act in the crisis. Crises.
We don't separate off from the consequences
of our imprint, the fall of forests we grew up
in and around, we heard so much about. It all stops
or struggles on, and the head reels trying
to get a fix on where we are in relation
to where we "should be". I am making
decisions – or pre-empting decisions.
The forests of the world are disconnecting.

JK

46. *Almost there*

I propose that joy is the aborted thought. Rude?
Not in the old Jamaican way of naughty or
slack — ah, rudeness! Delight is at the shore's
edge, before the ocean, the eating of food
before the defecation. You have pursued
the slick stoney path towards the spray and roar
of the waterfall, only to arrive where there's no more
sparkling spray, no cooling mist, no desire, but the lewd
messiness of lust. Delight does not like extremes.
It settles in the in-between, it hangs
in the well-lit closet where everything seems
ordinarily pleasant. Joy lives before the pangs
of regret, of the tragic death of dreams.
Somewhere in there, life withdraws its gleaming fangs.

KD

47. *At a stretch: 16 lines*

I was worried about the local crops
in the way I have been worried about crops
since I was a child riding the tractor
on the farm, since I searched for answers
in grain silos, since I worked "on the wheat bins",
and since I disc-ploughed the stolen
ground for wheat and oat seeding.
This worry was part of processing
contradictions between eating and being *de trop*.
I was worried about the local crops
because of the long hot dry weather —
the young corn withering, beans pods under-
sized, and oats wilting. Then storms
brought vigour at last moments, and storms
corkscrewed into sections to make empty patterns,
and storms unleashed further contradictions.

JK

48. *Suburban Theology*

It's a foolish dog barks at a flying bird
                    — Marley, "Jah Live"

How do I explain the way that a certain cult of kindness
can be nothing but the glow concealing the lie
of a culture still harbouring the canker of its sins –
the way a nation is built on shed blood, the way
the scribes construct a myth of righteousness,
a myth of holiness – the Darwinian logic, the toughest
thing to counter: We are above you because we won,
and we won because God made us win, and God
made us win because we are right, and you are wrong.
This is a doctrine that must be rushed over,
leaping over the chasms between each clause,
the solipsism of their logic of decay – Christ
offering his wry ironies and wit as a midwestern man;
and all the women are pioneering Mormon types,
tenderly coy, but submissive as women who know
the value of their magical whiteness, the type
who've mastered their seduction of tears and smiles,
indulgent necks to the clumsy heads of soldier men,
valiant as militia troops, promise-keeping types;
the suburbs of America, lifted and transported tourist
elegance of the stretches of Israel photoshopped
for Christian pilgrims – all convenience,
white and noble and familiar – how whiteness
carries a culture, a way of seeing the world,
how the lovely, the faces of symmetry, the selected
looks of these disciples, crafted in the sexual fantasies
of the thousands, the millions, and this is the truth:
that the faces of Black people are on the periphery,
and this is the art of triumph, the art of war.
I last feared the end of times when the two sevens
clashed – the sensation is the same as awe tinged

with terror, a rapidly darkening sky over the grand
impossible stretch of landscape arrogantly
stolid against the hubris of engineers.
Today, the European plains are aflame,
and at 3:00 a.m. this morning, St. Louis' skies
opened to the rainiest hour in history – the deluge,
crawfish as large as lobsters shuddering out
of the drains. Are these the last days? asks
the prophet; and why, he asks, are there tears
in my eyes, despite my robust scepticism? It is
how they have us. First, the bombardment of heat,
the sweet in the milk, the scent of acid in the air,
and the electric storm rushing over the Rockies.
I have not heard from my sister in weeks – not the dead
one, she is always whispering and chuckling – but the one
who must be staying indoors in London, hoping
for the heat and the rain, more and more rain,
the blessings of God, the curse of God. I have not
heard from her in weeks, and I think of her
on this day of heat – the Lincoln index one hundred
and two degrees, the sky as impervious as ever.
We are all the chosen ones, it seems, despite
our geographies of anthills and savannahs; we are
the chosen, sandalled and robed, eating berries
and ants and speaking our tongues inconveniently,
our dark defiant skins as offensive as truth.

KD

49.

Something *good* from the realm of settler
delusions, maybe, just maybe, Kwame.

From the realm of settler delusions
that is the country of Noongar

people. The realm is the survey,
fencing and selling by The Crown

and those it protects, works alongside.
Country is the sacred land of its people.

The *good* is in a moment that set itself
against the realm and asserted country.

No saviours in any of this, but a seguing,
even a coming together across almost

two centuries of crisis. Mountain to hill.
Not the only coming together, but still

a coming together around a river.
With Marion Kickett, a Noongar Elder

of great wisdom and knowledge, I shared
space and we spoke against the realm,

spoke for country, and for healing
and reconciliation. I followed her lead.

I can only follow. I learn as I follow.
We made a statement together. We sang

together. It was intense. The river was listening
and I learned to hear it. I dissolved into words.

JK

50.

And this little tendon strain
to the hip is a soft pain

I massage daily — this, *I learn
as I follow* — the sincerity

of it, the kindness of it,
and for me, its unknowability.

For when I ask myself how do you
follow, I return to the peace-

keeping child, stuck in the middle,
hungry to see what comes next,

and what we have left behind.
And this, maybe, is a kind of following.

My doctor says, Stretch the tendon
and it will be well, I promise.

So, I believe him, and stretch
the tendon, oohing in delight.

It seems, then, that we must
return again to the solitudes of mortality,

caught in that middle place, the point
where the seer is cursed with sight.

2

I have stolen a toolbox of solitude
from the careless writer,

she who comes across accidents
of grammar and waits

for the finicky copy-editor
to correct them. I sit at the foot

of the table and wait for the discarded words
to hoard in my toolbox of solitude,

where I keep the record
of my silences, and where I rehearse

the end of all this. It is always
said that for the blessed

and ancient, the passing is peaceful,
surrounded by family and friends.

One imagines the lovely light
of early morning spilling

over the body, and something
like grace filling the room.

What is not said is that this singular
moment is the last sliver of solitude,

the grand emptiness of abandon.
The dying are as messy as the strange

contradiction of selfishness:
we arrive with nothing and alone,

and we return alone. The ignorant
writer is the blessed one.

She does not know the endings
of poems until the idea and meaning dry up.

She is, I mean, caught in the middle
way — full of beginnings and endings:

a metaphor, a flourish of language
or a forced understanding. And then it ends.

KD

51. *I was asked if "clichés had a place in poetry"...*

I expect changes in the body,
but that doesn't mean I am untroubled
by them. Last night in the *awake hours*
I decided on a series of "changes".
(a) I am going to subsist more on tea.
(b) I am going to start the summer
vegetables early because planting times
have been eroded if not *tossed out the door*
where seeds can't find purchase anyway.
(c) I am going to *get out into the world more*
even if it's in a different way from the old ways;
even if it's for only slightly longer forays
(sure, meant in the sense of foraging for sustenance
and not as a military metaphor) –
though I will miss the creatures I know
by unspoken names and worry about
how they'll get through safely in the valley
without an advocate, though maybe
there are others who play such "roles"
I don't know about... plus see end
of this poem that "refuses closure".
(d) I am going to get the changing mole
on my face checked this coming week
just in case it's *taking a turn for the worse*.
(e) All of these statements exist somewhere
between aspirations and resolutions,
but have qualities of "commitment"
about them and (f) Involve family
because I do not operate unilaterally,
though sometimes I lapse into solipsism
which I don't actually respect and draw
myself out of, a little embarrassed –
apropos of which, in this house
I am not the only advocate

for the creatures – there are three
of us, and each gives as much
as the others in this. The collective!
But I've a responsibility for my own body
and my own platitudes, and something
has shifted and needs shifting again.
There was an earthquake yesterday.
Tracy felt it and I didn't.

JK

52. A Prelude

I imagine my prelude would be where fear ended
like the end of innocence and the handsome
child, the toughening of skin, and the loathsome
terrors of regret, the dark guilt that contended

each day with a carefree mind. The soul's wound, unmended
by prayer, festered. I'll tell you a secret that only some
know, I was fostered by fear not beauty's ransom,
not the healing of trees. I am now offended

by memory that intrudes, asking me to endear
myself to that lost child of too many tears,
the boy who found rhyme with Felix Randal

during that season of the heaving JC years,
me as iron-shaper, Ogun among my peers,
striding the blast, in dusty pants and ragged sandals.

KD

53. *Scraps*

I kept two scrapbooks of space exploration
when I was a child – from the late '60s
Apollo missions through to Skylab. America.
They vanished when I was in my early 20s.
It's not a matter of memory to say that I pasted
cutout newspaper and magazine articles
onto the pages with homemade flour-
and-water glue. My mother had used this
formulation back in her childhood of the '40s.
The scrapbooks bulged till they flopped open.
Exploration wasn't a closed book. It had
consequences – foreseen/unforeseen. Space
vanished when they vanished, or it folded
back in on itself sometime during the early '80s.

JK

54. *The seventies*

[it is art] that speaks to the awesome process of becoming
— Rex Nettleford

We did not choose the country or epoch by
which we were made. The decade filled our backpacks
with the contraband of revolution, black,
as we knew our hearts to be – our hungry eyes.
devouring the genius of our heroes who would ply,
us with dream song. Soon we coveted the livery of lack,
we were our own deep-thinking, righteous Jacks
and Jills of the struggle, sending coins to glorify
the wars in Southern Africa, our little bits of fire
that we hoped would multiply and cause war to vault
the Boers' Bastille. Every dream in the skin's desire
reminded me of my own strength. Yes, I found fault
in my wild and sinful happiness, but I was no liar,
I was awake, smelling my body's musty salts.

KD

55. *Address to a white 'revolutionary poet' amidst a room of followers*

Peace is more radical than all that conjuring
of violent revolution, of all those correctives
and reckonings, all that myth-making
among like-minded company. Within
those fossil-fuel-loving Molotov junctures,
you join arms with the oppressors
via an adoration of their tools, and sign
a manifesto that declares there's only this action,
this response. But hunger and bleeding
is never exclusive, and the weapons of murderers
can only be weapons of murderers.
A cult of images is still the bombed-out building.
To be killed by police is to be killed.
To be killed by retaliation is still to be killed.

JK

56. The choiring of congregations

After the rituals of travel – the vaccinations, the visas, the photos –
we arrive, unsettled at heart, our feet swollen, our limbs aching.
Searching for comfort, as one whose body consumes
space, I envy my father-in-law's quiet efficiency. His body
slips into small corners, settles in the world, a sliver
of being, though his light glows. Here he can be seen
and not seen. I scowl, I carry the trail of my person behind
and before me, and the slower I get, the wider my spread.
In sleep, I conduct the inventory of my body:
the stomach's acids; the ankle's ache; the dense vertebrae
somewhere below the skull that, when pressed, causes
the world to lurch; the sins of weight; the tendon on the left thigh
sharp against my brain. I dream the promise of ease. Then I wake
in another country, gather my zip-lock bag of plastic containers –
the pills, the pills, the pills. In a hotel room, I luxuriate and stare
at the harmattan from the height of comfort. How easily I can
cloister in the assurance of the data unfurling in small, tiny,
manageable bytes. I conduct my labours from a phone and a cluster
of screens. We step out. I have never been here before,
not like this, and yet it all seems familiar: Accra stretched out
like Kingston, the pace of bodies speaking a dialect of slopes
and dances that are ancestral of skin and hair; the way the air
cools suddenly in the shade, the small comforts of the scent
of frying plantains and caramelized fresh sweet starches
and the composition of light in the sudden irrevocable sunset,
and the deep, consuming calm of night, the city slowing to highlife's
cadence – the choiring congregations swirling in the soft air.

KD

57.

Tim has been telling me about Accra since he was six
years old, though he has never been there.
For him, it wasn't an act of imagination, but of necessity.
It answered questions he couldn't even begin to ask
where he was. And we might connect with the *everyday*,
Kwame, without having been there before,
or "not like this; and yet it all seems familiar".
A whole series of actions of body, family, sleep,
medicine, organisation, the effects of light
and shade – and in saying this I don't think
I am repeating what you've told me. Apropos of.
Our long dialogue doesn't give me permission
to try to imagine myself walking alongside you –
I won't use Google images or Streetview.
I am not interested in satellite reports
or the demographics of various official
bodies or quangos. But I know some music
of that city (care of Tim), and I know some stories
that have reached me – writer to writer, poet to poet –
and I can imagine and smell a frying plantain.
And, Kwame, I can smell the ocean! Even
inland, on the "opposite side of the world",
I can smell the ocean! This is the resonance
of life and the hollow a vast body of water
makes as it encounters a coast, a city, biographies.

JK

58. A hall of revenants

Travelling again, I am running into
my revenant – the body remakes itself
in new landscapes – perhaps, as I have said,
not new, but different. For two years
my body has grown used to its stable
order – its shape and presence – and then,
in the disquiets of travel, I relearn my contours.
I have not admitted to many things outside
the jungle of my words – the constant
sorrow of what is left of desire, the hunger
always for light, consuming light,
and the disquiet in my body tender
as an old wound to the clipped
syntax and phonemes of Afrikaners
speaking English. There is such music there,
muddied by the tainting of memory,
the films, the lectures, the stern official
at the airport, the twitchy maitre d' questioning
our presence at the buffet. We land on the last
stretch of land before the Cape of Good Hope
and I await the scrutiny of my papers
with terror. It has been an uncomfortable
passage, my body still holding in the news
of fit, grinning Biyi's sudden passing.
And my fingers relish the tender memory
of my aunt Povi's slender hands,
as one longs to retain the sensation of last
touches, the feel of affection in skin on skin.
Her elegant face, the gardenias in her scent
welcoming me as the prophet in the hotel lobby:
"Oh, Kwame, oh Jesus, and Kwame, there is always
one – our prophet!" and me thinking, say, "poet",
though I am tempted by the hubris of prophecy;
the desire to see and see further, and then speak.

It is hard to tell if she is admonishing me
for my failure to fulfil all promises.
How age humbles us, how beatific her smile.
And my latest secret is found in the narrative –
to be told how to face my last days.
The problem with this aging poet is the way
all my metaphors are crowded out
by the plots I devise of my- deaths.
I make two vows today, as we circle
Johannesburg: never economy, not any more,
for my name is Oga, Nana Kwame, and I must
fly with the comforts of an elder – this,
and the more difficult, to make poems
of the beautiful things fiercely in their height
of oblivious delight – the persistent things.

KD

59.

We are still close to home, Kwame,
though the world reaches us in all its
    contradictory ways.

We are still close to home, but move about
regionally, recording changes that take place
    as if out of sight.

Today, a moment of beauty is reconfigured
in medias res: a white-faced heron lifts
    out of a roadside culvert

to wing over the eerie yellow of a genetically
modified crop of canola – *PIONEER*
    on the scarified land.

We are still close to home, Kwame,
but abstracting the images of here
    to build a montage

of a tense and fragile humanity
trying to piece things back together,
    just as it continues to dismantle.

In our heads, tracking the river
through the valley, it doesn't congeal
    into platitudes but rather

troubles senses, thought processes –
epistemology as much as ontology –
    the egret graphic against

a shallow but deeply reflective
hyperbola of paddock water
    seems like a pose or a cliché,

but that's only per a closed-circuitry
of comparatives — it can't be these,
   and it's more glorious than us.

JK

60. *A different knowing*

> *...and reconfigure into a different knowing...*
> John Kinsella

You are rehearsing my death again. The flame,
you fear, will be snuffed out soon, and the "Be wells",
by the well-meaning and kind, while the last bell's
sound, will be small mercy. It's best not to name
it, this macabre preparation, but it's the same
old ritual: your long departures, your need to dwell
in some teeming city, to walk alone while casting spells
against the curse of wasted years and all love's crimes.

I say nothing. There's no appeal bench, no justices
to plead my case; after all, I did sin. Grace
is what you have given me copiously, so this
is nothing to begrudge, this unspoken quest for a place
of peace where the body learns to find bliss
in the mountain of loss you know your soul will face.

KD

61. *Sunfish*

A young and record-seeking sailor's yacht
tussling with the Great Southern Ocean
has capsized after it apparently
hit a sunfish. This has brought
on another round of mockery
and abuse from media mocking the sun
fish as a ridiculous creature that has
no purpose. There's a popular rant
from years back calling them
"floating garbage" that has memed
its way into received wisdom — a giant jelly-
fish-eater that is brainless. The negligence
of its biological analysis aside, it's no Swiftian
"A Modest Proposal". But the glee is extant.

JK

62. *Pettiness*

In Memoriam, Milan Kundera

How sadly mundane seems his life, despite the throngs
of humans conjured in his books made to appeal
to the literati. When laid out in neat rows, the feel
of this obituary is lightness. The writer my wife read for long

hours when she lived in London during those strong
years of our making — he who wrote with a great deal
of disdain for a woman's love, yet could reel
out seductive prose, while I would get it all wrong —

is dead. I have envied his urbane wit, and where
I clambered though ruins of fanciful dreams, poor heir
to that generation of revolutionaries willing to turn
their bodies to martyrdom for the cause, his bare
prose held her enthralled. He is dead, I say, and wear
my false regret as some newly-formed concern.

KD

63. *Reading war propaganda in failing light*

Through the burn, light diminishes
rather than increases. The shutters,
down till now to drive it back out, are opened
to drag it back in, to show paths and roads
through angled speech, forks where
no branches follow. When we are here,
end light is so close to first light,
though we fall into an earlier form of night
as the wind shakes the Schönbuch
and the city, and isotopes forsake
their shapes, their geochemistry.
It has to get to this point, doesn't it? — trees
shaking, insects shutting down, a dive
into answers that are scripted, optative.

JK

64.

> At Keyla, the village of the great masters, I learnt the origins of Mali and art of speaking. Everywhere I was able to see and understand what my masters were teaching me, but between their hands I took an oath to teach only what is to be taught and to conceal what is to be kept concealed.
> — Mamaudou Koyate

Anyidoho, the prof, moves with a slow shuffle
these days. It has been a few years, but
the weight of years grows heavier. Still,
his hunger for this art is the same; the man's
gentle calculations unfurl between long pauses.
His body grows still as if he is transported
to the seaside, the glittering water, the scent
of earth's beginnings filling his nostrils – the poems
travelling across the void. This is the griot's haunting.
His patience is an art. We gather in his office,
two translators, a spectator, and an facilitator.
The red, dirt-stained whitewashed walls, the deep dark
grotto of these buildings – it is Jamaica, again;
Legon as familiar as Mona – the squat colonial
buildings, the sweet scent of villagers' cooking
wafting through the window, the voices of a people
continuing to live the life of earth and sky.

The translators wait for his pronouncements;
the pause between breath and utterance
is reverence. When he declaims his poems
in Ewe, the room gathers in a kind of awe,
and the translators join him, as if rehearsing
ancient prayers, their faces beaming with knowing
and all poetry becomes a mothering tongue,
a closed calculus of meaning and sentiment,
a courtyard of livid green discovered

in the middle of a calamity of stone walls.
It is the cool water required to quench the thirst
of all long-travelled prodigals. I do not speak my mother's
tongue, but carry its music in my body, the soft
consonants, the sea swell of vowels, the hum
of contemplation. In this moment, poetry is limitless,
it seems, and I know nothing, though I feel everything.

KD

65.

My father has been taken to the acute ward.
His leg is swollen with infection, his heart
isn't working, and they're keeping him alert
to the world with pints of blood. In a metric
system I get stuck on this — one unit, one
pint... 8-12 pints in the body... oxygenated.
He is 85. Last year he had a stroke. He
came through and now this most private
of men is expecting family to arrive.
We are on our way. It is today. Almost now.
We speak the same *language*, but are
always translating; it took decades
before we realised that was an answer.
But it happens automatically, 'til we
pause to think about it. The degrees
of love and affection, the complications.

A shining bronze cuckoo hunting down
caterpillars struck the house and stunned
itself. It hunched on the verandah
trying to find a way back. We watched
through a window, wondering when
to step out and help. But slowly its
head began to move, then quicker.
A shimmering blue beetle I'd released
from the house earlier rocked by
and the shimmering bronze-green
of the cuckoo remained still. The
beetle enacted its transit. Then, as
I was about to go out and cradle it,
place it in a box to warm into activity,
it was gone. Shortly, we will drive
down to the city where Dad has been
transferred to the acute ward. I repeat

myself, overconfident; poetry gives
me permission to do this. He'll be
thinking through the pain, and anguish
about the football. I know this for sure.
We will see him soon. One by one.
And what's in me of him will tremble
so slightly it won't show, because
that's the way of the Kinsellas,
that's the affect of past exiles.

JK

66.

The landscape rises noisily at the Cape of Good Hope,
and all the gleam and neatness of vehicles and glass-
glittering buildings — the ritual modernization of the planned —
burns to destroy each year the intrusion of alien species,
though all the stamp of our human order is silenced
by the crash of the waves against the rocks
and the rush of the wind across the face of granite,
a biblical calamity of clouds and constant storms
here on the Cape of Storms, the Cape of Wrecks,
the Cape of Good Hope. At the Maiden's Cove, Easton,
the guide, asks me if I will go to Robben Island. I shake
my head, and he is not sure I know, so I say softly,
"I am not fit for the trauma", and he loses the decorum
and banter of the good tourist guide, grows deeply sombre,
and nods, "I understand," he says. And so we carry on
to the lighthouse and the stormy chaos of the edge
of the world. It is as if I have a tenderness in me, the fish
bone under the skin, the heavy throat of sorrow. And here,
Aba comes to me — her beautiful face, her laughter,
her wisdom, my anchor — and I'm back, days before,
at Cape Coast, the chaka-chaka of the houses and the narrow
streets, the gutters, the lanes, where I wanted to ask her,
"Do you remember Mammy's house? Is any of this familiar?"
Half-expecting her to tell the driver to stop, to lead us deep
into the crowded streets of bodies pressed against each other,
her mouth running a mile a minute, until we arrive
at the place, and her saying, "Here, right here." The driver,
though, turns into the parking lot beneath Elmina Castle.
"Will you go in, Uncle?" "It is too much," I say. "It is the sorrow of it."
We have been returning generation after generation,
and each journey forward is a journey backward into memory.
Back in Accra, I consume a mountain of hot kelewele,
the Legon breeze caressing the body like memory.
I am talking poetry with Kofi Anyidoho, as he eats banku

and okra stew. Aba, you would have asked for more kelewele,
and we would eat, and eat, and remember. So today,
I carry tears beneath my skin. I don't push aside the heavy.

KD

67.

In this to & fro of ours, Kwame, of such long
standing now by way of poems, and maybe longer
in a sense of connections and what they can
and can't mean, I read your distress and I "work
through it" in ways that aren't compartmentalised,
aren't sure of themselves, are never certain. And it's not
that I adapt or that my way of understanding adapts,
no, rather it's that every moment of heaviness
is broken down into fragments or strands
or fibres that different parts of me might
work through. And it's not an array of analogies
and similar experiences and like for like,
and even where there are overlaps, they
are so different it just doesn't seem right
to say I understand, because this equates.
The language of poetry is infinitely
limited as well as infinitely variable.
I know what I am trying to say,
but letter after letter won't let me
say it. It seems more like a set of sounds,
an array of symbols I don't recognise
but know I have created, so I might approach
the resonances, the echoes, the reverberations.
But I approximate nothing. What can I *say*
out of *thinking*, at a moment of distant "sharing"
that wasn't? What can I write that coheres?
I lapse into story but not anecdote, I hope.
When I was a child I plucked unripe
banana "fruits" that hadn't formed
into anything *identifiable* because they
grew in a place where only the outer fringes
of unformed, barely unfurled leaves reached the sun
over a wall – it being neither the climate
nor the place for a banana tree – but I took

those stunted nubs of fruit and offered
them up to my mother for cooking,
because I'd read somewhere that in other
climates… only to be told (gently, warmly)
that they weren't actually plantains
that could be cooked, could be eaten,
and I went back to the banana plant
in its eternal shade among building debris
and laid those fruits down, believing
they would bring more trees
and that these would carry
the sun in them, needing
no help from outside.
In this to and fro of ours,
Kwame, I travel away, but close,
and hope that's not intrusive.

JK

68. *Grace*

Then one morning, three weeks after the dance,
they stop calling her name. Then comes a form
of sorrow. We leave Nebraska where it is still warm
and land in Panama where the soft glance
of the casual passerby carries the countenance
of a village, and from the hotel, a quick storm
smudges the line between sea and sky. A swarm
of good feeling circles me. I do not want to chance
the return of sorrows, do not want the heavy stone
of fear to consume my gut. The only known
terror of night I have is the fear of her face
slipping away — her leaving. You see, I own
nothing, and have no spells against being alone.
I know now it's not love but fear that's wanting grace.

KD

69. Thames

> "Near where the dirty Thames does flow"
> — William Blake

There's a big poem I want to write about the river
but it refuses – the OXO tower wrecks me – and it involves
my artist grandfather, a Londoner, who had to leave
for Australia when he was twelve. That's so often
the thing with children having to leave the familiar –
'had to'. What comes of such alienation is a manner
of painting and a manner of looking back – forced
as consequence. His father died under a train
in front of him. I only have Blake's "London" in my head
which is an obfuscation. It involves bridges. Flood defences.
There's a world ecology that messes with locality.
I claim nothing, but being there is also obligation.
There's a big poem I want to write about the river,
but it's about gulls, opacity and equivocal resolve.

JK

70. *Soldier*

That the history of a poet's mind is labour
Not unworthy of regard, to thee the work shall justify itself.
     — William Wordsworth, The Prelude

There are then those, like us, who seek to bless
our tribes with songs we hope will do their part
in tearing walls of the self-loathing heart
to rubble. Ah, but this is the great vanity, I guess.
After all, poets must abandon poems for war
to be useful in revolutions. Which makes us less
than workers, but indulgent purveyors of our art,
trading in the currency of prizes that smart,
careerist writers win. We say "self-express"
as if that is *the* sacred right, a way to break through
the despair and doldrums and find bliss
in the freedom of speech to say, "Me, I must do."
Well, I say, "To hell with you, old tyrants, you can kiss
my soft ass. And with your tweets, likes and to-dos,
you can kiss my other vulnerable parts, too!"
I won't stop singing, I'll keep on doing this.

KD

71. *Shout*

I am walking from the bus stop to the flat
when a couple of "young blokes" passing
in a car slow down and shout abuse at
me. I turn and study them – curving
around a corner, they slow further
and shout again. I shake my head and disappear
down a lane-way, wondering if I will
find them waiting at the other end.
This happens to me around the world
for no obvious reason. I don't get their angle.
This weekend Tracy and I will march
in the Pride Parade to show our support –
there have been harassments and countermarches
by conservatives here. We will sing but won't shout.

JK

72. The birth of tragedy

The famous singer — the mouth of gravel
and growls, thick with the dialect of cities
of Dutch-Italian immigrants, shaping their ownership
of the New World, blood on their hands, a people
who carry their wounds as invaders as marks
of their humility — he grips his guitar, bends
over the microphone and, nervous in New Orleans —
caught between heir apparent and the hot new thing —
he sings, "With these hands, with these hands…"
Who has blood on their hands? The man from the hills,
arriving with the news that God is dead, is who.
And prayer is the light of hope, even in the squalor
of history, that broken, flawed people can make
heart and love. Is this poetry, is this Marley filled
with spirit, telling people, "Don't let them fool you",
his right arm outreached forward, over the Red Sea,
over the multitude, over the bodies, before
"No Woman No Cry", sung to the stranded,
the exiled, the shipwrecked, the townships of Cape Town,
the streets of sorrow, the bodies broken with blood
hardening, the battered, the broken, the earth's wounded?
To say a poem can sing outside the body of the poet
is to say much about poetry, and yet in moments
like this, the poem is all that matters — the tears of words
shaped in tongues, the hollow sound of feeling:
"Let it sing, let it sing, let it sing." With the rock singer,
the poem remains, the holiness of the moment
remains. I have considered the depth of my faith,
feeling perhaps that it may be stronger than hope,
for I have never wondered, in seeing the suffering
of the world, where is God. No crisis, no dark night of the soul.
The dead will be with us. The suffering and the wounded,
the drowned and the lashed, the enemies of my peace
are before me each day. The calculation of the wicked

is enough for me, and the hum of comfort is my tender
incense of opium — my comfort, my peace
after a day at the ramparts, after the marching,
the bending of the world to my vision. "Eventually,"
Andre of Port au Prince chuckled, "eventually, even
the revolutionary must sleep, must repose, must pray.
Even those with the blood of God on their hands, must rest,
and the streets will be bare — the roads free for us
to move through, to find safe passage home."

KD

73.

I have been troubling over poems
I once wrote that take to task Griffith's
Birth of a Nation because though they pull
it to bits and lambast its contents,
just the mention of its existence
is enough to make me reel
and reconsider. But can his
horror be forgotten, given
there is an ongoing soundtrack
and cascading images
that flow well beyond
the time and place and duration
of the film? In asking a hypothetical
question of the "director", as to how he
would have cast, say, Marilyn (in black and white)
if she'd been a contemporary actor,
and if she'd been willing,
which she might not
have been — whether he'd birth
or rebirth her as black or white
within his construction of origins — I was trying
to undo the journeys of cinema so easily
taken by opportunists such as Tarantino.
Further, in the state of a nation whose states
implement "legal lynching", who poison
and electrocute, who gas and discuss
best possible ways to execute, who keep
the documentation of demise
in their digital archives, with newspaper
reproductions from *prior* a kind of vintage
ephemera or memorabilia, I see nothing
as having changed. I have to keep
writing such poems, or trying to. Consider

the demographics of who is killed
by the state and who does the killing.
The state vs. the consequences of state?
There's no poem long enough
or compacted enough to carry
that paradox. There's no finishing
line to reach – it keeps moving.
And there's vast room for "atmosphere",
for private profit – the icons
of white culture-making
keep updating and being updated
so they can ensure the executions
keep on flowing – legally sanctioned,
threaded through "history",
defining a life span,
the length of a song
by Leadbelly: "Folk-tales".

JK

74. *The maximilist poets*

Oh dear friend, what have we done,
we, the maximalist poets of this epoch?
And yet to think of erasure and diets
of choreographed silence, the quaint
efficient clipping of soul and dreams,
the embarrassment of abundance
held back, seems like a kind of failure.
We dare not fail the pressure of words.
The burning hijabs, the smoke,
the shattering monumental gestures
of those who place their voices
on the rack – the risks they are taking –
tells me that we must rail against
the acts of the ignoble and wicked,
they whose acts chew away at the icecaps,
celebrate the dark-stained bones
of the dam now drained to mud,
how monstrous is their terrorizing,
how easily they map the path
of our destruction. Must we not
find a poetics that spills
out of all these broken things
as they rise up in our bellies?
What we do is what we must do
until we can do no more.
I confess, though, a gratitude
to the TLS reviewer who read
us as arriving at the word "lean"
for how we find each other.
We might say love or mercy?
But it's all the same to me,
a way of being seen and being
heard in these dark times, my friend.

KD

75.

Here's the strangest thing, Kwame,
prior to that review I had started writing
a series of "minimalist poems" that carried
"maximalist" mirror responses. This came out
of a discussion with Tracy about the present-
day drive in some ambits for "maximalist"
design. These synchronicities arise
out of "discourse", *indubitably*, but they
are also sparks across the valleys
and chasms, across the open
and closed spaces. On their own,
they mean nothing — just moments
of momentum and inertia
in acts of writing and publishing —
but in acts of trying to announce,
trying to register, trying to bring attention
and scrutiny, trying to affirm witness,
trying to listen to many conversations
and to one conversation, trying to record,
trying to argue, trying to analyse,
trying to pray, trying to critique,
trying to share, trying to offer support,
trying to acknowledge, trying to respect,
trying to shout, trying to whisper,
trying to make more of poetry than item
or object or ingredient or object or collectible
or product or commodity, we need to reach across,
we need to come together, we need to harmonise,
we need to counterpoint, we need to take our own stories
and intertwine with other stories; without taking away
from those stories we need to speak and listen.
We need to make room for noise, we need to make room
for silence, we need to build with each other without
damaging what is already there. We need to pass through

the vegetation and over the water and through the cliffs
without damaging. We need to translate and know when
not to translate; we need to pause and leap; we need to do so much
in our poems and with our poems together alone together…
and we are this, Kwame, as well as the things we do and write
apart – solo – all that and all the other interactions
and sharings… all those words and gestures
that make our lives… all that and the more they contain,
all that and this, too, our way of saying alongside
each other, speaking with and through and to
but always together, finding space
where space has been taken or closed off,
and sharing, Kwame, sharing… yes,
that "one love", that "one love",
and the endless multi-voiced love
that is one, too, is one, too, and many.

JK

76.

I can say what I want, you can say what you want,
but someone betrayed by blood is someone broken.
They can be forgiven for not returning to tender, to care,
to take them down into the catacombs
of the old precinct on a Friday, sightless and stumbling,
without the promise of a quick release.

To forgive is to forgive history and blood and old
betrayals, a father's casual abandonment of a boy,
the pain of it, the numb keloid of it is all we have to offer.
This man has said, "I grew up fatherless. It happens."

A win of sorts, but with too many rules and permutations,
of sentiment and consideration. The compromises of love.
"If this, but that, if it is and wasn't," says the sage in the bushes.

And so, here is the chasm I cannot bridge – this haunting,
this fear of such absolute assurance in one's rightness,
I will understand only as one understands death and decay.

KD

77.

How we step across those chasms or fall,
wondering when we'll hit the rocks
which come quicker than we think. There

seem to be no "bottomless" pits. It's
been grass-cutting here, and a broken
toe and a rock-strike on the steep

rocky slopes, on the broken lines
of hillside. But none of that prepares
me for what just happened now —

doing foot-laps around the house,
in and out of the high UV,
wearing thongs — that's flip-

flops in American orthoepy — when
I hear a deep rustle like the rubbing
of bricks together, and look down

and see a thickset five-foot dugite
ss-ing past, breath and tongue close,
to press closer to house before

cutting across brick paving and through
wire mesh into a fallow vegetable bed.
Dugites have one of the deadliest

venoms in the world. I wrote an elegy
for the last person who died of a dugite
bite in Western Australia — the wife

of a friend. Dugites pursue mice,
and this is their mating season.
It is their time in the valley.

Yes, a deep rustle like the rubbing
of bricks together. In and out of chasms
like they were designed for it,
as adaptation predicated.

JK

78.

Thrice this week, I must send condolences to acquaintances
whose intimacy has grown the more by empathy – we are of an age
of sudden deaths, or the prolonged and painful passing of loved ones.
It is fall, and I know that we are all, in our small boxes,
dreading the dusk, knowing that trees turning orange and crimson,
will be, for years to come, the way we will see our losses
our complicated loves. So, when I write mycondolences,
I scour the poets I trust – I know, at once, the inadequacy
of my own poems – how clotted they are with the details
of pedestrian news, with private names and anxieties.
I find Grimay's "Elegy", and note she has not said who is dead,
has described a lone hawk as an image of how we move
through the world longing for what we have lost.
I think how generous is the open-endedness of her sorrow,
how fitting to send to my three acquaintances,
so they will find themselves in the fall sunset reading
into their grief a kind of beauty. Yet I regret even this gift,
in the way, of late, I have regretted my body, the cupcakes
I devoured, their sour residue on my tongue, my blood
betrayed, my waning lusts; regret the sprawling words
written in journals years ago, that list of things in the moment,
without a hint of how they record time passing. What remains
is gratitude to Grimay, and her "Elegy", and the gift she offers me,
wordless in the face of what I know is to come, has come,
and will continue to come: night time, and the long, long sleep.

KD

79. *Before the Eulogy*

My father is dying.
My father's wife
has asked me to write
the eulogy. I will.
My father has asked
that I don't return
to Australia for the funeral.
He is happy I have work
and wants things
to remain as they are.
He is not seeing people
in his last days.
He refuses medication.
We grew around each other
over recent decades,
and that won't stop after.

JK

80. *Before mourning*

I stay bated all week as if waiting for the flue
of sorrow — an elegy or eulogy, for the lank
body of the bereaved. It is unfair, a kind of shank
pushed in when we least expect it, when we fall to
weeping and wail lamentations through
the nights. Perhaps to sorrow now is to be sunk
down into loss while the air is still rank
with the glorious stench of living. We do
inure ourselves from the future of waist-
banding, hand on head, sackcloth and ash, hair curled
in unruly neglect when all we do is laced
with threads of grief. Your news has hurled
me into acts of prevention, this race
to master sorrow before true sadness unfurls.

KD

79.

I do not know how to write an elegy for a teenager
who was murdered in the streets of Midland.
I do not know who to write an elegy for a teenager
who was already a leader in his community.
I do not know how to write an elegy for a teenager
who loved Halloween and looked forward to yesterday.
I do not know how to write an elegy for a teenager
who got off the school bus with his mates and was beaten to death.
I do not know how to write an elegy for a teenager
who was chased and racially abused before being held down and killed.
I do not know how to write an elegy for a teenager
who, senior police say, was "just in the wrong place at the wrong time".
I do not know how to write an elegy for a teenager
and find that *right place* and *right time*.
I do not know how to write an elegy for a teenager
whose family are grieving and will fight to stop this happening again and again.
I do not know how to write an elegy for a teenager
who is one of many Aboriginal people murdered by white racists.
I do not know how to write an elegy for a teenager
who was so essential to the health of country, the world.
I do want to know how to speak out. I do want to know how to step
out of a colonial society that would have us enable it behind the scenes.

JK

82. *Elegiac*

For Kojo

Eventually what remains is all head, the sculpted
dignity of a face, beautiful in its authority,
the lips, the smoothly embossed eyelids, the jutting
noble forehead. I am startled by the relief of me,
what I will become, dear brother, what we all
must become, the body waning away to bone and tautness,
the pounds you have lost, the beard, a mercy of texture
and grace – how neatly she has trimmed it for you,
carving out your beauty, white against mahogany.
Your body is the case that holds the arteries that circulate
the weekly cleansed blood, the machine pumping, rituals
of fatigue and more fatigue, and then some relief
on the third day – a space to let the muscles rest.
You are wearing those dark expensive shades –
you've always liked the finer things, the classy. Call it
stylish blindness. You are myself returned to me in the ways
we understand need. Kojo, my embrace expects
the gathering of sullied flesh, but I feel me consuming
your fragile bones – what you have come to, what
we have come to. All that remains is the beautiful head,
this gloriously formed creature – the animated dignitary
defying the posterity of the heroes' gallery,
the pedestals of busts lining the walls like the spoils
of barbaric wars. Seeing your face is not so macabre
but something endearing as an old comfortable revenant
returning to me the nobler shadow of my too, too, solid self.
There is no language for this mourning before the news.
Still, we who are cursed with the good fortune of years
have learned to rehearse the heavy sorrow of our loss.

KD

83.

The crisis of this land
was written in the face
of the helicopter pilot
as they manoeuvred
their machine so close
to the house, so low
over the valley it splayed
trees and sent wild
animals scurrying.
I looked them straight
in the eye. I looked
as the earth shook
and they existed between
air and crashing down
on ancient country.
The household was
traumatised. Tracy
rang the ranger and
it was not on the record.
Take a photo, but the
photo op had passed.
The valley breeze
cannot reset and the dirt
and rocks and aquifer
can't rest, levitated. Clearly
another mining operative
scanning the old for new,
to trace minerals they
can brag of to a world
ready for products,
eager to turn a blind eye,
to consign elegies to other
places. This is what comes
before the drills. What comes

before the eco surveys
that sign off. For the good of.
Weighed up. On a Sunday,
in the calendar of the West.
On a Sunday morning
when possible storms
didn't develop.

JK

84.

...Soul's case...

> For Yusef Komunyakaa

Mid-November and the air is brittle, the cold
is an old friend. She waits at the corner,
impatiently, then smiles coolly as I arrive;
grasps my hand, and pulls me along the leaf-whirling
avenues. "Look," she says, "at the topography
of this place; soon the snow will cover it all,
and you will forget the stanzas of your walk.
We must call it the long, long sleep."
And, cheerfully, she sprints ahead, her skirt
a flurry of yellows and ochres, the hint of red
to ward off demons, flashing just so, as she turns
the corner. I hurry to catch up. She is gone.
The sky is blue. This seems prosaic, and yet
if you saw the blunt truth of its immense blueness
you will understand my grammar — blunt as an essay.

So here, also, is the agnostic prose poet, the one
who knows the foul hubris of the French who contrived the ledgers
of slaves bought and sold, the *Code Noir* and the *Code
Blanc* of privilege. Every chemical is translated from
the Latin, the catalogue of insects, the secret listings
for breadmaking and the grocery list of the street cleaners'
union. Everything spoken in the language of Gauls is poetry, they say.
So Komunyakaa comes to the prose poem
with caution — he's seen the trigger of a booby trap in the jungles
of Cambodia, the tenets of what carnage it does,
the way blood turns to dust — the only word he has
for the spray of flesh and blood — to think it is poetry
we speak of. He says, *Write everything.* He says,
Then, force it into a corset, yank tight

the straps, let the spill fall off, discard, make
verse of paragraphs — each line an event, a machine
of events, carved into humble and correct
lines. He says, *Trust lines. Then collapse them*
into paragraphs. This is the prose poem I make, I trust.

English is diabolical, a language of coins and calculations.
English cankers into the stony absolutes of decrees,
the sentence pronounced, the fractioned bodies.

These rooms I make are soul cases, says the poet.
These rooms I make are the cases for the souls.

I return to the corner, now bundled in the efficient
fabrics of the winter, and I look for her. I even wait,
feeling dumb and dangerous, a loitering black man
in a neighbourhood where movement is my safety.
She does not come. Though she does, in the blue
of the sky, in the coinage, "the soul's case", that I ponder.

KD

85.

New neighbours down the road
and they're removing old-growth trees.
It's agony. Distress has so many registers,
but it is always distress. I have been
standing with my arms spread, hoping
the birds driven from the collapsing
branches might find their way across
the ravine to me. Across the firebreaks
and paddocks, from that zone to this.
Mum and her partner have Covid.
Mum is mid-80s and they are both
given anti-virals to augment
their multiple vaccinations.
I am thinking of them as I stand
out "in the elements", a human tree
trying to simulate lushness and reliability,
my cambium layer building cell by cell
to accommodate the influx of displaced
birds. Fugitives in their own valley
contemplating a perching, roosting
and maybe even nesting future
on this anti-scarecrow, this narrator.
Reliable, unreliable, distressed.

JK

86.

...*Before the darkness*...

For Stephen Kuusisto

The blind poet still has the dog, and where it was all blackness,
now he can see through a tunnel of one eye.

So, he blows up his words until he can see the shadow
grow still. At the lip of the Museum of Art, a tall lanky

handsome Black man, fit as an athlete in his sixties,
stops me; the tapping stick makes me imagine how he got

this far. I say I am off to the museum; he points to the museum
and says he's looking for a diner. Do I know one?

I say there is one down the road, and he knows to point his
hand for me to say, *Yes, where you are pointing*, and as he goes

he says, "I am Charles." A beautiful man, and I keep
thinking that I have seen my mother and brother

and read the letters of my grandfather
and heard my mother speak of her father – all the blind ones –

and keep thinking that God is bringing shadows
my way and I am reluctant to learn, though I want to ask,

Do I buy a stick before the narrowing of light
or do I wait for the gloom of my soul? Can I prepare

for this? I avoid Charles in the museum,
but promise myself to come to him next time, like I did with Jesus

in Kingston — all those near-meetings, all that avoiding,
all that terror in the face of the peace-promises of lifted burdens.

These days I am open to the assistance of ancestors,
thinking then of the old Lome man, my grandfather, how much like

an ancestor he seemed then, when I was barely able
to know enough beyond the mood of a courtyard,

the sour taste at the edge of porridge sweetened
by roasted groundnuts. He, I think, will have doctrine

enough to come among me and tell me how to meet
the darkness. Or perhaps the sculpted face

of Levi Dawes might return to meet me for the first time;
my other grandfather in Kingston's darkening jazz streets.

The thought occurs: if we are going there, why would we
not allow that they have been among us already? There

is comfort in that, I suppose, the way that the ancestors return
to be healed by our blue open hearts, our hungry need.

KD

87.

This is a day when your "being out there"
makes all the difference for me, Kwame.
    I read your poem and journey
with it, if not with you. I am not limited
to my own perceptions, care of your grace

and generosity. Your poems increase me
as prayer or contemplation does, and in
    other ways that transition across
language, across topographies
and demographics. I see remarkable

things after reading them, disturbing
things after reading them, and follow
    the branching roots of each line
simultaneously. Sky, people, and earth.
Lives encountered and recounted.

And on this day when your "being out there"
makes all the difference, we here contemplate
    the months to come — said to be the worst
summer before it has even got fully under
way. Each day we prepare until we are at its end.

We've known each other long enough now, Kwame,
to note the variations in repetitions, the way
    cycles loop over themselves and entangle.
We know the limits and incredible
expansiveness of action, and we know

each other's atmospheres of mortality.
Every poem is a surprise and a confirmation.
    Every poem is the one that follows
and starts our conversation over again.
This pattern holds it shape, then doesn't.

JK

88.

I became handsome, irresistible,
when I grew impotent, as if all sap
left my balls and spread a smooth
oil over my body, my tongue, my mind.
The bruja prescribed herbs and Viagra,
though she warned, "You will grow ugly
again, tough and gnarled. Your god,"
she said, "is a god of ironies, your curse,
holiness." And I grew angry.
She laughed and said, "Just love yourself;
it is free as air. Love yourself." Which is
easier said, though I did not say it,
as I have been practising the opposite
of complaining these days, though falling
short of contentment. How slow and assured
is our body's decay. In these times I repeat
myself in self-portraits, a thousand selves
echoing themselves. And I seek to discern
the changes. But there is nothing,
just the boredom of repetition, so intense
that I whisper under my breath, "Were I
to encounter my face on an autumnal street
of golden light, I'd pass it by,
wondering at the strange apparition
of a black face in this neighbourhood."

Imagine, then, this song:

Argentina

Little by little, this race is becoming extinct...
The race is losing its primitive colour in the mixture.

It becomes grey. It dissolves. It lightens.
The African tree is producing white Caucasian flowers.
>Juan José Soiza Reilly, "Gente de color"
>in Caras y Caretas

This is my lurking nightmare, though,
if asked, I would demur at the hysteria
of it. Instead, I leave slivers of verses of alarm,
lamenting the disappearance of my face
in the nooks and crannies of civilization,
while I, ironically handsome, impotently
stumble along the familiar avenues
in the slow arrival of the first winter storm,
the earth growing faceless
in the startling, blinding blizzard.

KD

89.

I think of myself as being of one place
and others think of me as being of another –
I shouldn't be surprised, not because
of where they're coming from, but what
I make of where I am. Moving
further way from my body,
moving closer to a void
of speech markers, I sign
my confession with water
though the pressure sensor
is failing and the pump unable
to give to the plumbing what's stored
in the Great Tank. There's a two or
three day wait before a technician
can journey from the city to repair
the unit. I restart and restart in burning
sun or by torchlight. This is the absurdity
of my asseveration, which I've never
actually believed in. But another
snake didn't bite me a few days ago
on the verandah, and I still sense
that I know where a particular southerly
wind began – that point over the sea
around Antarctica, that overclaimed,
unclaimed continent I also
shouldn't be part of. This body,
trying to keep in touch so moving parts
can keep in shape, so water
with a touch of the entire biosphere
in its make-up might anoint me
"purposeful", "relevant", medicinal.

JK

90.

God is the lack of the world
   — James Dickey

With care and an improvisational hunger,
we surmise that God is what the world lacks, which
sermonizes with too much desperation, so we turn
language to music, reach across language
and borrow the verb *faltar* – that which is needed,
lacking, wanting, longing. God is our lack,
our lack is god, the world lacks and lacks
the blood of need, the hollow of absence
in this darkening season. The shadows on the plains
are the mesh of need on the body. The sun
is blunt, it holds over the snow-covered land,
and still at the edge of a year's ending,
it is death and the lack of those we have lost,
and the fear of the long winter of ailment,
which is what fills the lack. So, *Amen!* says
the barking geese in the sky that lacks hope.
The season falters – the void of our daily rituals.

"Had it not been for the fall," says the preacher.
"We would not squabble over stale bread."

1968
A white poet in Dekalb County Georgia speaks to a tribe,
and they applaud with the exuberant delight
of people welcoming, with relief, their hero,
the one who never denied them in the cities.
The poet is not in mourning, in tune with gospel
laments, turning around the red earth, the cortege
moving with the slow procession of sorrow,
with flame in its wake. The poet is at peace.
Slaughtered kings do not bloody his verse.

He has seen too many dead: the deer, the soldier,
the wayward vagrant, the idler, the nameless.
Too many have died on foreign soil. And the tribe
is desperate for its talismans. The chivalrous dead.
"Swinburne is dead. I am now the king of the crumbs.
I am now the king of the falling crumbs."

Don't eat it? It's stale. Are you trying to shame me?
So now you'll go out into the streets and say,
Look at my life. I married her and she feeds me stale bread.

This is the last of the bread. After this, we will starve
on water and then we will die. The toaster is still
working. Let's toast it and cover it with oil.
It will be better, tastier, don't you think?

It will kill you. It cannot kill anyone. It's good
for breadcrumbs. You eat breadcrumbs all
the time. It's never killed you. Why do you
think I want to kill you? Do you think I won't
just walk out and leave? What type of love
do you think I have for you? All I feel is staleness.

So, if I soak it in water, well, okay, if I sprinkle
it with water as in the way of the sacrament,
not immersion, not the burial – too crude,
too much of African in the blood – will it be fresh
again? The world is starving. No, we are starving.
This is all we could harvest outside the grocery store.
It was not gangrened. Just like this – stale. We need it.
It is healthy. It is the mercy of God. If I bring
a decanter of wine, and you break open the loaf,
share it with me, and we drink the wine,
and eat the bread; it will be as holy as newly
baked bread – perhaps, less so. It will cleanse our souls.

I am wading through the swamp of the Georgian
white man's accent, thick as terror,
knowing that there are sudden
reverberations of meaning. Difference is there,
and so is the depth of the language
and the revelation that spoken words
give off that which they do not need.

KD

91.

It is many years since we've been down
at Serpentine cemetery where Tracy's brother,
who died at eighteen, swimming in a Hills dam,
is buried. We visited yesterday. It was hot
and cicadas were resetting tenses,
recalibrating the chronology of lives
above and below ground. Not long
emerged from their subterranean
nymph-lives, they rise like sap
out of roots, and marri-tree foliage,
exuding a calm volatility. Forty-two
years after his passing, Tracy stands
on the verge of the grave, and the loudness
of cicadas shifts understanding.

JK

ABOUT THE AUTHORS

Kwame Dawes is the author of over thirty books, and is widely recognised as one of the Caribbean's leading authors. He is the Glenna Luschei Editor of *Prairie Schooner* and a Chancellor's Professor of English at the University of Nebraska. His latest book with Peepal Tree Press and W.W. Norton is *Sturge Town,* which was a Poetry Book Society Choice. He was born in Ghana, grew up in Jamaica and has lived most of his adult life in the USA.

John Kinsella's many books of poetry include *Jam Tree Gully* (WW Norton, 2012), *Drowning in Wheat: Selected Poems* (Picador, 2016) and *Insomnia* (Picador, 2019). His newest collection, from Arc Publications, is *Brimstone: a book of villanelles*. He has published work in all genres and across a few of them as well, and collaborated with many artists, composers, writers and poets. He is a fellow of Churchill College, Cambridge University, and Emeritus Professor of Literature and Environment at Curtin University in Western Australia. He acknowledges that he lives and works on stolen Ballardong Noongar country, further acknowledges this land was never ceded, and is committed to the full return of this land to its peoples.

ABOUT PEEPAL TREE

Peepal Tree Press has been decolonising bookshelves since 1985 with our focus on Caribbean and Black British writing. We are a wholly independent publisher and part of the Arts Council of England's national portfolio since 2015. In 2024, we established a partnership with HopeRoad Publishing.

Peepal Tree's list features fiction, poetry and non-fiction, including academic texts and creative memoirs. By the end of 2024, we will have published 490 books by 320 different authors, including those published in our anthologies. Most of our titles remain in print. Our books have won the Costa Prize, T.S. Eliot, Forward, OCM Bocas, Guyana and Casa de las Americas prizes.

From the beginning, women and LGBTI authors have been fully represented in our lists. We have focused on the new by publishing many first-time authors and have restored to print important Caribbean books in all genres in our Caribbean Classics Series. We have also published overlooked material from the past as a way of challenging received ideas about the Caribbean canon.

We see decolonisation as about overthrowing and repairing oppressive, economically exploitative and racist power relationships. Many of our books explore the halting, difficult process of overcoming four hundred years of colonialism in the Caribbean in the post-independence period. But we also see decolonisation as needing to happen in Britain. We are committed to ending British amnesia over the destructiveness of empire and colonialism, including our role in the irreparable damage of nearly three centuries of slavery , and promoting an understanding of how Britain's long relationship with the Caribbean has contributed to the making of British society in ways that persist into the present. As a publisher, we have taken a stand on supporting Palestinian rights for freedom from a colonial occupation and denial of statehood.

We hope that you enjoyed reading this book as much as we did publishing it. Your purchase supports writers to flourish. Keep in touch with our newsletter at https://www.peepaltreepress.com/subscribe, and discover all our books at www.peepaltreepress.com, and join us on social media @peepaltreepress